· · · · · · · · · ·

Complaining, Teasing, and Other Annoying Behaviors

Complaining, Teasing, and Other Annoying Behaviors

• • • • • • • • • • •

Robin M. Kowalski

Yale University Press
New Haven and London

Table 2.2 copyright © by Robin M. Kowalski

Designed by Nancy Ovedovitz and set in type by Binghamton
Valley Composition, LLC. Printed in the United States of
America by Vail Ballou Press

Library of Congress Cataloging-in-Publication Data
Kowalski, Robin M.
Complaining, teasing, and other annoying
behaviors / Robin M. Kowalski.
p. cm.
ISBN 0-300-09971-1 (alk. paper)
1. Interpersonal relations.   2. Interpersonal conflict.   I. Title.
HM1106.K69 2003
302—dc21   2002153573

A catalogue record for this book is available from
the British Library.

10 9 8 7 6 5 4 3 2 1

• • • • • • • • •
Contents

Preface

When respondents to a survey were asked what they considered most important in giving meaning to their lives, the majority singled out their interpersonal relationships. When they were asked what caused them the most stress, dissatisfaction, and disappointment, their answer was the same: their interpersonal relationships. How is it that the most important source of meaning in our lives can also be the source of our greatest distress?

A large part of the answer is that at times people are annoying, unpleasant, and downright mean to one another. Strangers, co-workers, friends, family members, and the loves of our lives alike frequently behave in a wide variety of ways that annoy and distress us. They mercilessly tease us, embarrass and humiliate us, complain incessantly, constantly worry and seek reassurance, lie to us, betray us, and put us down. These ways of behaving are not merely annoying; research has shown that they can have disproportionately disturbing effects on our mental health and on the quality of our relationships. Offensive encounters make us feel unloved and unwanted. Dissatisfaction with personal relationships is one of the primary reasons that people seek professional therapy.

This book explores in depth annoying interpersonal behaviors in six categories: complaining, teasing and bullying, egocentrism and arrogance, incivility and breaches of propriety, worry and reassurance-seeking, and deceit and betrayal. These behaviors represent only a small sample of the annoyances we face as we go through life, but much of the discussion applies to other types of offensive behaviors as well. What sort of people engage in them? Whom do they select as their targets? Why? What are the consequences of these behaviors? Perhaps most important, what can we do to minimize them and their harmful effects? Unfortunately, we all are exposed to other people's annoying behaviors. In truth, we all behave in annoying ways ourselves from time to time. This book is intended to shed some light on why we humans behave as we do and to suggest what we can do to make our interactions more pleasant for other people and for ourselves.

Aside from the authors I cite, the names of the people I quote and of the people they mention are pseudonyms. Their stories have been minimally edited for clarity.

Several people deserve special recognition for helping me complete this book. Amber Hardison provided me with innumerable insights into the topics discussed here. Much of the material on narcissism and reassurance-seeking reflects her input and helpful suggestions. I am also most grateful for her generous help in research. Mark Leary once again provided extensive editorial feedback. He painstakingly read the entire manuscript and was willing to bounce ideas around and to listen to my gripes about deadlines. My parents, Randolph and Frances Kowalski, spent many hours baby-sitting to free my time for writing, and their many words of encouragement were more helpful than they know. I am very grateful to them. I also thank Western Carolina University for a leave that allowed me time to write much of the book. Barbara Salazar deserves recognition for her extensive editorial work on the book. Finally, I thank Susan Arellano and the staff at Yale University Press for their help and enthusiastic support for this book.

1

• • • • • • • •

The Offensive Side of Social Interaction

The things people do that annoy and hurt us can remain lodged in our memories for years, even for a lifetime. The incident that Carla relates is trivial, but she's unlikely ever to forget it:

> When I was in high school, I rode to school with Beth. She also picked up my best friend, Susan, and Dan—who could be rude and obnoxious. Dan always had chewing tobacco in his mouth, a habit I found disgusting, and he always spat in a bottle—even more disgusting. . . . One sunny day as we sped along the highway with all the windows down, he decided to spit it out the window. He was in the front seat and I was in the back seat right behind him. The tobacco flew from his mouth out his window and right back into mine. . . . At that moment I was laughing at something Susan had said. The dip hit the side of my face and ran into my mouth. I thought I was going to throw up. Dan turned around and laughed and all I could do was gag! I never even got an apology.

Karen's recollection is more hurtful:

> Years ago, a friend and I planned for weeks to go to a college basketball game. He said that no matter what happened, we would go. He was of great importance to me, and he would never

let me down. At least, I thought he never would. He called me at the last minute and said that there was a family emergency and that he could not go. I still wanted to see the game, so I found someone else to go with. At halftime, I went to get a drink and I saw him with another girl. When he saw me, he knew that I had caught him. He had lied to one of his best friends. At that point, there was nothing he could say to make me forgive him.

Allison is still troubled by hurts inflicted on her in grammar school:

Teresa ruined my self-esteem my first three years of school, and it made a lasting impact on the way I handle confrontations. Teresa lived in my neighborhood and was three years older than I. She decided that I was a threat because little Tiffany down the street adored me and Teresa hated it. So she got the neighborhood kids to go along with her in continuously teasing me, tricking me, and excluding me. She made me cry virtually every day. To this day I don't understand what I ever did to her to make her torture me for three years. I was angry at her for many years afterward because it made me feel inferior all through elementary school and to this day.

Stacy is being made the butt of behavior she finds not only annoying but infuriating:

I have an acquaintance who has more job experience than I do and likes to talk about how easy things are for her and how she hates being instructed in how to do things she already knows. I have no job experience in my field and have a hard time dealing with the way she flaunts her superiority. I feel that she puts me down and belittles all the stress I have in trying to learn and study. When I don't understand something, she says "Duh" and "Well, obviously."

Amy, a recent bride, has heard all the complaints about weddings she can tolerate:

One thing that always gets on my nerves is a constant complainer. I have a friend who is always complaining. As we were driving down the road one day, she began to talk about her wedding. She had just attended mine and began to complain about long ceremonies. She said people were just stupid to have so many songs, and then poems on top of them. She said the preacher shouldn't talk long. She also said that her wedding was short and that everyone enjoyed it more. She never said it, but I knew she was implying that my wedding was awful because it was quite long. She made me really mad, and I haven't asked her to ride with me since.

Diane found herself suffocated by a boyfriend who needed constant reassurance of his importance to her:

I used to date a guy who went to school in Atlanta. We would see each other about every two weeks. I was happy at first, but then he began calling every day and wanting to talk all the time. He was on break for a few weeks and constantly asked my permission to go anywhere. I hated this. It wasn't even like we had been in a serious relationship, and he was treating me like we were married. When I graduated, he made a special trip from Atlanta to see me, and then followed me around all day. I couldn't even spend one of the most important days of my life with my friends because he wouldn't quit following me around like a little puppy dog. He constantly needed reassurance that I was happy and he was good enough. He offered to change his complete life around for me. At this point, I told him I needed out, and I didn't want to date him anymore. He hasn't spoken to me since.

What, if anything, have other people done to annoy you today? Make a list of all the annoyances that immediately come to mind. Do any of the incidents on your list resemble the complaints of these young women? Now think about what you have done today that might annoy others. Make another list of those annoyances.

Looking over your lists, notice what types of behavior annoy you. Are you annoyed by complaining? Teasing? Rudeness? Dependency or excessive seeking of reassurance? Betrayal? Lying? How do these behaviors make you feel? When people betray you or lie to you, do you feel hurt or humiliated? When you are teased, do you enjoy it or do you find it hurtful and troublesome? How do you typically react to such behaviors? When you behave in these ways toward other people, do they typically react the same way you do? Why do you complain to other people? Why are you sometimes so dependent on your significant other? Why do you do these things when you know the effects on other people are not likely to make them want to clasp you to their bosom?

The behaviors that trouble us typically occur within the context of our relationships with family and friends. The old saying that we only hurt the ones we love has more truth to it than we may think. Although it may seem ironic that we would choose to behave in ways that annoy the people closest to us, it is that closeness that gives us the freedom and security to let our less desirable selves show. Closeness, however, also makes the troublesome behavior hurt all the more. When an acquaintance lies to us or cuts us off in conversation, we may be temporarily annoyed, but we don't experience the same degree of hurt that we feel if a family member or romantic partner does the same thing. John Amodeo (1994: 10–11) summed up the situation well when he wrote that "the knife of betrayal cuts most deeply in our close friendships, intimate partnerships, and committed marriages. These relationships contain our greatest hopes, while being the source of our deepest hurts."

The Frequency of Annoying Behaviors

Depending on the quality of your own relationships with friends, family members, and intimate partners, the frequency with which people behave in ways that annoy the people close to them may or may not surprise you. If your relationships with family members and friends are courteous as a rule and low in conflict, you may not quite realize how common many annoying behaviors are. If your relationships are generally full of conflict and annoyances, you will not be at all surprised to hear that "on any given day, 44% of us are likely to be annoyed by a close relational partner. . . . On average, young adults encounter 8.7 aggravating hassles in their romantic relationships each week. . . . Most people (66%) get angry at somebody in any given week . . . , and every seven days most young adults will be distressed by different encounters with a lover's (a) criticism, (b) stubbornness, (c) selfishness, and (d) lack of conscientiousness, at least once. . . . Over time, people are meaner to their intimate partners than to anyone else they know" (Miller, 1997: 15). It appears, then, that annoyances are an inevitable part of our everyday lives.

The frequency with which people engage in annoying behaviors really shouldn't surprise us. Any time two people enter into a relationship, whether a friendship or a romantic partnership, they bring to it their own needs, expectations, desires, and relationship histories. It would be unrealistic to expect that the needs and desires of the two individuals will never conflict. The more time two people spend together and the more intertwined their lives become, the more likely it is that conflicts and disagreements will arise. In addition, over time people become more comfortable and secure in their relationships, and consequently exert less effort to please each other. Persons who were once careful to pick up after themselves, for example, now leave their clothes lying on the floor for the other person to pick up.

Such patterns of relating suggest that our interactions have always been marred by annoying behaviors and that the annoyances we experience today differ little from those experienced by past generations. But is that really true? Have people always been as rude, disrespectful, and hurtful as they are today? Or have changes in society and technology altered the ways we interact with one another? Are complaining and teasing more common today than they were three or four decades ago? Do people today have more difficulty withholding comments and behaviors that may hurt or offend others? Are people more chronically dissatisfied with their relationships and jobs than they once were? Are we more likely today to betray and lie to our partners because we expect more satisfaction from our relationships than our parents did from theirs?

Although the answers obviously depend on the specific annoyances being examined, in general it seems that people *are* more annoying and disrespectful than they were just a few decades ago (Miller, 2001). One reason is that, at least in Western society, people's expectations have changed markedly over the past several decades. Technology alone has led us to expect that things will move quickly and that products should work faster and more efficiently than ever before. We seem to feel more of a sense of entitlement than people once did. Our attitude is "What are you going to do for me?" When our high expectations are not met, we become disappointed, angry, and hostile. Unfortunately, we often take out our anger on the people closest to us. A man who has a bad day at work seldom goes into his boss's office and complains about it, but as soon as he walks in the door at home, the anger pours out.

In addition, either because societal standards have become lax or because people themselves have become daring and brazen, we see more and more people who do not hesitate to do and say things that were once considered grossly inappropriate. We are so frequently exposed to belching, flatulence, and swearing that they no longer shock us, although behaviors we accept in an adult may still be unacceptable in a child.

In view of the changes that have taken place in our world, perhaps we should be surprised that annoying interactions do not occur more frequently than they do. Perhaps, rather than focusing on all the little white lies our friends tell, we should be surprised that they manage to tell the truth most of the time. Rather than focusing on our mother-in-law's seemingly endless complaints, we should pay attention to those times when she doesn't complain. Though standards for appropriate behavior do appear to have become more lax over the years, we can attribute the civility we also encounter to self-control. According to Roy Baumeister (1997), annoying behaviors reflect a breakdown in self-control, a loss of the inhibitions that once held such behaviors in check. It is not so difficult, then, to understand why people behave in ways that offend others; the difficulty is in understanding why they choose to behave appropriately as often as they do.

Still, some people seem to be more likely than others to behave in ways that offend us; and some people are quicker to take offense or to perceive malice where none was intended. What is it that makes some behaviors appear to be offensive?

Factors that Influence Offensiveness

How offensive a particular behavior is perceived to be depends on a variety of factors, some of which have to do with the perpetrator, some with the victim, and some with the situation. Some general factors that influence people's perceptions of annoying behaviors are their basic psychological needs, their desire to save face, the ambiguity of the behavior, whether they are the victim or the perpetrator, the repetitiveness of the behavior, any apology or other reparations offered, nonverbal cues, the intent behind the behavior, the victim's perception of the behavior as an indication that the perpetrator does not value the relationship, and the actual nature of that relationship.

BASIC PSYCHOLOGICAL NEEDS

Behaviors are obnoxious to us, in part, when they interfere with our basic psychological needs. We all have needs that must be met if we are to experience a sense of well-being: the need to belong, the need to maintain our self-esteem, the need to feel in control.

The need to belong is so basic that some psychologists consider it a key human motivation (Baumeister and Leary, 1995). The need to be accepted by others is so strong that it drives much of our behavior. Although the strength of this need varies from person to person, everyone wants to be wanted and dreads being excluded. Any behavior that somehow threatens this need is perceived as troubling and offensive. Good-natured teasing that is perceived as an indication of liking and camaraderie will be enjoyed, but malicious teasing threatens the victim's sense of belonging or inclusion and therefore is hurtful. Similarly, some betrayals, such as an extramarital affair, leave one person feeling rejected. A lie, however, may be resented but will not necessarily be hurtful unless it threatens a person's need to be included.

When people feel excluded or rejected, their self-esteem shrivels. Mark Leary and Deborah Downs (1995) suggest that our self-esteem serves as an indicator of the degree to which other people include or exclude us. When we feel rejected, our self-esteem is low. When we feel accepted, our self-esteem is high. Because people generally want to feel good about themselves, any behavior that leads them to feel excluded is perceived as unpleasant.

Some behaviors may also interfere with our need for control. For example, a friend's chronic lateness threatens our sense of control when we are repeatedly wasting our time waiting for him. Again, people vary in the amount of control they feel they need. Some people's need for control is very high, others' not. Even those who have much less need for control, however, don't want to feel out of control, particularly when that feeling is caused by another person's behavior. Bullying, egotism, and incivility make all of us feel out of control, so we take a dim view of them.

Even though we consider behaviors annoying and obnoxious when they interfere with these basic psychological needs, it is often our attempts to satisfy those needs that prompt other people to engage in the annoying behaviors in the first place. A bully's desire to maintain a secure place in his peer group, for example, may prompt him to put others down. By putting them down he exercises control over them, and in the process increases his own self-esteem. Thus the needs to belong, to exercise control, and to maintain self-esteem that prompt bullies to put other people down are the very psychological needs that become threatened in the people they bully.

LOSING FACE

In any particular social interaction, people turn a face to the world—a particular image or impression they want to convey. When anything causes us to feel humiliated or embarrassed, we are said to have "lost face." In other words, we have failed in our effort to convey the image of ourselves that we want others to perceive. Think of a time when you tripped and went sprawling. Even though you may have hurt yourself, probably the first thing you did was look around to see if anyone had seen your ignominious pratfall. If someone did, typically you'd feel embarrassed because you had temporarily lost face.

Needless to say, maintaining face—or facework, as it is sometimes called—is very important in social interactions. When people lose face, social interactions become derailed. Neither the person who has lost face nor other people who are present know exactly how to respond. In fact, maintaining face is so important that some researchers believe that maintaining one's own face and helping others maintain theirs is an inherent part of social interactions (Cupach, 1994). In other words, most people, most of the time, don't even have to think twice about trying to ensure that both they and the people with whom they are interacting are spared embarrassment and humiliation.

Yet some people do intentionally say things to make others lose face. Erving Goffman (1967) captured the essence of the hurt inflicted by people who have no compunction about causing others to lose face when he characterized them as "heartless."

Concerns with maintaining face may lead people to perceive even polite behaviors as annoying or offensive. Some people, particularly men, perceive compliments as condescending or fawning. Similarly, a victim's response of "I forgive you" may be seen as offensive if the offender doesn't recognize that she has done anything that calls for forgiveness (Exline and Baumeister, 2000).

AMBIGUITY

Although the intent of many annoying behaviors is quite clear, others are so ambiguous that it can be difficult for a victim to know how to interpret them. Was he teasing you to share a joke with you, or did he mean to hurt you? Was she intentionally rude, or was she simply not thinking? Was the braggart really trying to put you down by making himself appear much better than you? The answers will obviously affect your feelings about these behaviors and about the people who inflict them on you. If you tell yourself they had no intention of hurting you, you'll be able to take their behavior in stride; if you assume they did mean to hurt you, your feelings toward them will be as hostile as you perceive theirs to be.

Typically the ambiguity that is so troublesome to the victim is advantageous to the perpetrator. Ambiguity allows perpetrators a way out when they realize they have gone too far. They can always say, "I was only kidding!" They can even compound the offense by saying, "Can't you take a joke?" Similarly, a person who produces an offensive belch can say, "I couldn't help it." Regardless of the behavior, perpetrators can always escape responsibility by saying, "You take things too seriously."

WHO IS DOING THE PERCEIVING?

Like beauty, annoyingness is in the eye of the beholder. How annoying you perceive a particular behavior to be depends on whether you are the victim or the perpetrator. Perpetrators are often surprised by their victims' negative reactions to their behavior. A person who plays a practical joke may be shocked by the anger of the response. After all, the perpetrator was "only kidding."

Research has shown some very specific ways in which victims and perpetrators differ in their perceptions of obnoxious behaviors (Baumeister and Campbell, 1999). The victim sees the annoyance as part of a pattern of behavior that has been going on for a long time; the perpetrator sees it as a momentary response to annoying behavior of the victim. Victims rarely think they have played any part in provoking the behavior. It may seem to a perpetrator, for instance, that a victim has set herself up to be teased by dressing in a way that seems outlandish to the perpetrator but totally cool to the victim.

Differences in the way victims and perpetrators interpret annoying behaviors become very clear when the roles are reversed. I have always been a practical joker. The practical jokes I play are intended to be funny and I generally don't carry them very far, so I am always surprised when my victims fail to see the humor in them—until the tables are turned and practical jokes are played on me. I'm afraid I dish it out far better than I take it. The way I interpret my own practical jokes is altogether different from the way I interpret practical jokes that other people play on me.

Victims even differ among themselves in the intensity of the annoyance they feel. Much depends on the strength of their needs to belong, to maintain self-esteem, and to feel in control. The stronger those needs, the more likely one is to rate other people's behavior as offensive. Similarly, people who tend to have strong emotional reactions to other people or who are sensitive to signs of rejection will be more inclined to interpret even innocent behaviors as hostile. So will people who have suffered rejection or disrespect in the past. Many people whose family and friends repeatedly lie to them will react more negatively to a lie than people who have seldom been lied to.

REPETITIVENESS OF THE BEHAVIOR

The effects of a person's history with particular behaviors suggest that the factor that does most to make some behaviors annoying is their repetitiveness. People seldom object if someone who rarely complains does occasionally gripe about something. In fact, people who never complain may be viewed more negatively than those who complain once in awhile, possibly because people who never complain are viewed as secretive. Similarly, people who are guilty of rudeness now and then are viewed less negatively than those who are repeatedly rude and disrespectful. Occasional improprieties are typically viewed as accidents or as caused by the situation; frequent improprieties have a much more deliberate quality, so the person is more likely to be held accountable for them. Similarly, most people are more willing to excuse an occasional white lie than repetitive lying.

Researchers at the University of Louisville have proposed the term "social allergen" to refer to a behavior that has become extremely annoying as a result of the cumulative negative effect of repetition over time. Your physiological response to a physical allergen—an irritant such as dust, say—is usually minor at first. With repeated exposure to dust over time, however, you may develop a full-blown allergy. The mechanism is the same for social allergens. A few exposures to rude, annoying, and obnoxious behavior have a relatively minor effect on you. Another person's occasional need for reassurance, for example, is unlikely to bother you. In fact, it may even please you. After repeated exposure to the behavior, however, you develop a full-blown social allergy— "a reaction of hypersensitive disgust or annoyance to a social al- lergen" (Cunningham et al., 1997: 191). It is repeated exposure to the behavior that makes it so annoying.

REPARATIONS OFFERED

The intensity of the annoyance aroused by a behavior is also in- fluenced by whether the perpetrator offers some form of repara- tion—an apology, a plea for forgiveness, or some other effort to make amends (Exline and Baumeister, 2000). Failure to follow rudeness by an apology is itself a breach of propriety: it reflects the offender's feeling that he is entitled to behave in any way he pleases, regardless of the consequences. When people are clearly repentant, "their actions may interrupt a downward spiral started by the transgression, replacing it with a cycle of positive intent and action" (Exline and Baumeister, 2000: 126).

Not that an apology will wipe the slate completely clean. The fact that someone who has been uncivil asks my forgiveness does not guarantee that I will forgive her, but I will be more likely to temper my anger in light of the reparation she offered.

NONVERBAL CUES

Nonverbal cues, such as the tone of voice in which a complaint is uttered or a wink accompanying a tease, can increase or mitigate the annoyance aroused by a behavior. Such contextual cues signal to the victim whether the behavior is intended as a serious threat or as a humorous interchange. Behaviors that are intended to be funny and are taken that way are obviously not viewed as annoy- ing. Contextual cues, however, can lead us to evaluate behaviors more negatively than we might in the absence of those cues. Peo- ple who look down their noses at us as they nod coolly in response to our friendly greeting simply reinforce our evaluation of them as egotistical.

Contextual cues may pose problems for the perpetrator, too. Some contextual cues are more difficult to control than others. The bully may find it hard to regulate his tone of voice and control the rigidity of his body as he maliciously teases someone. To the degree that other people pick up on these cues, the perpetrator will have difficulty excusing his behavior by saying, "I was only kidding" or "You take things too seriously."

INTENTIONALITY

The intent behind any kind of behavior plays a large role in the way we perceive and react to it. It influences the attributions we make for why the behavior happened and, subsequently, the emotions we feel. A behavior that seems to us intentionally hurtful arouses much more anger than one we attribute to sheer thoughtlessness. It would probably be safe to say that a large percentage of offenders do not intend to hurt their victims. Indeed, the realization that someone has been hurt is the most common reason cited for regretting a remark (Knapp, Stafford, and Daly, 1986).

People are much more forgiving of annoying behaviors that they perceive as intended to benefit someone other than the offender, as when someone tells a lie in an effort to protect a friend's feelings. In this case, the liar has little to gain from the lie but sees that another person stands to gain a lot. Because the intent of the lie is to do a kindness, people judge the behavior very differently than they would if they saw the intent as malicious.

Unfortunately, people sometimes misunderstand others' intentions. If they see malice where none was intended, they set themselves up for problems. A person who has been teased relentlessly over the years about his big ears, say, is unlikely to see any sort of teasing as a friendly gesture, even though the teaser may have actually intended to be sharing a joke. Someone else who has been raised in a family where teasing is an accepted, enjoyable way of interacting will be much more likely to see teasing as fun. She may even join in the teasing.

Misperceptions are more likely when someone's annoying behavior, although not particularly obnoxious, is simply the proverbial straw that breaks the camel's back, the one annoyance too many that sends us over the edge. Malcolm Gladwell (2000) refers to it as the "tipping point." Tolerance for behavior we perceive as annoying may depend in part on where it falls on the tipping scale. For example, an annoyance that occurs at eight in the morning when you are in a good mood will seem much more trivial to you than the same annoyance at five in the afternoon after you have just discovered that your car has a flat tire.

Perceptions of intent, whether correct or not, are also influenced by the very fact that annoying behaviors are negative. Negative behaviors are weighted much more heavily than positive behaviors (Coovert and Reeder, 1990). We rarely acknowledge other people's good behaviors because they are what we expect. That's why negative, annoying behaviors make such a big impression. Because we focus so much more attention on the negative than on the positive, the negative has a disproportionate effect on our emotions, our behavior, and our mental health.

PERCEIVED DEVALUATION OF THE RELATIONSHIP

The way other people behave toward us can convey their evaluation of our relationship. Behaviors that annoy or hurt us may tell us that to the perpetrator our relationship is of little value or importance (Leary and Springer, 2001). Perhaps more important than the perpetrator's actual evaluation of the relationship, however, is our perception of it. When we react to annoying behavior, we are reacting not to the perpetrator's judgment but to what we perceive it to be. When a perpetrator appears to accord the relationship far less value than the victim does—a situation that has been termed relational devaluation—the victim feels rejected.

People may feel rejected even when they have not actually been rejected. How many of us have felt hurt and rejected by teasing when the teaser was indeed only kidding? The perpetrator may be completely unaware that she has hurt the target's feelings. Teasers who really are motivated by an impulse to have fun and to establish camaraderie with the target are stunned when the target mistakes their good intentions for malice.

People vary in their desire for close relationships and hence in their sensitivity to indications of rejection. People who have little self-esteem and are extremely sensitive to rejection are more likely to interpret others' behavior as malicious than people who are high in self-esteem and relatively insensitive to rejection.

Even behaviors that seem positive to most people may be interpreted as negative. Consider politeness. Most people are raised to be polite and to treat others with respect, and in most situations they desire and appreciate polite behavior. But what of the people who interpret others' politeness as condescending and demeaning? Probably we have all known someone who has seemed to be unable to accept a compliment gracefully. If people view compliments as condescending, they will see a compliment as an indication that the person who has offered it places little value on their relationship. Such a misperception is particularly likely if the person who pays the compliment is of higher status than the target (Holmes, 1993). It's in our nature to want to be liked and respected. Any behavior that we view as indicating that a relationship is of little value to the other person not only makes us feel rejected but threatens to make us lose face.

THE NATURE OF THE RELATIONSHIP

The nature of the relationship between the perpetrator of annoying behavior and the victim has a large bearing on how annoying the victim perceives the behavior to be. A complaint by a stranger may be annoying, but you can easily dismiss it because you may never see that person again or can contrive to avoid her. Obnoxious behavior by your spouse or another family member, however, is a different matter. You cannot just turn your back and terminate your relationship with your spouse or your mother. You are forced to deal with that behavior. Besides, we expect the people close to us to have respect for us and for our needs. Surely they should know better than repeatedly to behave in ways we find annoying. We can forgive an occasional slight, but hurtful behavior that someone close to us repeats again and again becomes increasingly difficult to forgive.

We are not always, however, more annoyed by the behaviors of close friends and partners than by those of strangers. Typically the exceptions involve behaviors we ordinarily welcome. We are more likely to put a positive spin on a compliment from a close friend than on one from a stranger. If your boyfriend tells you how attractive you are, you will probably be pleased and flattered, and even wish he would make such comments more often. But if the same comment is made by a construction worker as you walk past a work site, you are far more likely to feel annoyed than flattered. Thus depending on the nature of your relationship with the person, a behavior that is perceived as flattering in one situation may be perceived as verbal harassment in another.

Uses of Annoying Behaviors

In view of the frequency of annoying behaviors, they clearly must serve some useful function, at least for the perpetrator, although their usefulness may escape the victim. That annoying behaviors can have some redeeming value may seem counterintuitive, but some positive meaning can be attached to virtually all of them.

ENHANCEMENT OF RELATIONSHIPS

Although it may be hard to imagine how annoying behaviors, such as complaining and teasing, could enhance a relationship, in many instances they are in fact designed for that purpose. Teasing may be used to establish camaraderie. Before people can tease others effectively, they need to know some things about them. Thus the very act of teasing conveys some degree of intimacy between the teaser and the target. In an effort to increase that level of intimacy or to demonstrate camaraderie, people often tease.

Similarly, complaining can be used to establish relationships with other people. Used in this way, complaining is sometimes a social lubricant or an icebreaker. You have probably found yourself waiting in a crowd of strangers for a concert to begin when one of them complained about the heat or the star's failure to appear on time. In such instances, complaining is being used to establish a connection with other people.

Dependency may also be a means of establishing or maintaining intimacy. Although after a time dependency and constant reassurance-seeking can become suffocating, they convey a desire for connection and intimacy. Indeed, many people who have been the targets of such behavior say that, at least initially, they felt flattered that another person needed them so much.

Even lies and other forms of betrayal may be perpetrated with the ultimate goal of enhancing the quality of a relationship. People may withhold information they fear a friend may find hurtful. Sometimes we tell our friends that they look great when in fact we can't imagine how they can bear to be seen in public dressed like that. Physicians may withhold information from a terminally ill patient or blatantly lie if they believe the truth will serve no useful purpose and only plunge the patient into despair.

In addition, annoying behaviors can often add some excitement to an otherwise placid relationship. Occasional breaches of propriety, however annoying they may be, are sometimes funny and allow partners to share a good laugh. Similarly, a complaint can often trigger a lively discussion. Thus annoying behaviors can add a little spice to life.

CONTROL

From the perspective of the perpetrator, annoying behaviors can serve the positive function of allowing the perpetrator to control or change someone else's behavior. When we are annoyed by the way others are behaving, we may complain to them about it, tease them out of it, or make them feel guilty about it. It may seem ironic that annoying behaviors can stop annoying behaviors, but they can be used very effectively in this way.

ENHANCEMENT OF SELF-ESTEEM

Perpetrators may behave in ways that annoy us as a means of making themselves feel better and thus bolstering their self-esteem. Although discrediting or putting someone else down serves a positive function for the perpetrator, it is highly annoying to the victim. By discrediting or putting someone down, bullies can make themselves look better by comparison. These tactics also draw attention away from the bullies' own deficiencies, again allowing them to maintain or even enhance their self-esteem.

A display of egotism may serve a similar function. Many people who behave arrogantly actually have a very low opinion of themselves—or, as some social psychologists prefer to call it, a fragile self-concept. They use arrogance to make others see them as better than they see themselves.

RELIEF OF BOREDOM

People may engage in behaviors that other people find annoying just to inject some excitement in an otherwise boring life (Baumeister and Campbell, 1999). Boredom can easily contribute to behaviors such as teasing and bullying. When people are bored, they seek stimulation. Kids who are bored and aimless may join gangs in order to have something to do with their time.

Of course, some people are more likely than others to become bored and more likely to seek relief in activities that others find troublesome. People who are high in sensation-seeking are the ones who go in for sky-diving or bungee jumping. They crave excitement and are miserable without it. This is not to imply that high sensation-seekers will necessarily resort to annoying behaviors in efforts to eliminate boredom; but they may well do so if they have little self-control (Baumeister and Campbell, 1999).

Targets of Annoyance

The frequency with which we are exposed to annoying behaviors and ourselves engage in behaviors that others find annoying suggests that no one is immune to the experience. Annoying behaviors are directed toward everyone. But that's not quite the whole story. Annoying behaviors are more likely to be perpetrated among friends, romantic partners, and family members than among strangers. In some of my research, almost a third of the annoying behaviors that people said they had perpetrated were directed toward close friends, almost a fourth toward romantic partners and family members, and another fourth against acquaintances. No one described targeting strangers.

I did find, however, that men and women differed slightly in the targets they chose. Men perpetrated annoying behaviors most often against close friends, then against romantic partners. Women, too, most often targeted close friends, but their second choice was acquaintances. Because, stereotypically, women tend to focus more attention than men on the nature and quality of their relationships, they may be more cautious about doing anything that may annoy their romantic partners. And when they do annoy their partners, women are more likely than men to apologize (Holmes, 1993).

Consequences of Annoying Behaviors

The consequences of annoying and hurtful behaviors are of course as various as the behaviors, the perpetrators, the victims, and their circumstances, but a clear distinction can be drawn between the consequences to relationships and those to individuals.

CONSEQUENCES TO RELATIONSHIPS

In view of the frequency with which we are confronted with annoying behaviors and the fact that most of these behaviors are perpetrated among people we are close to, it is reasonable to expect that annoying behaviors will have consequences for relationships. In rare instances, as we have seen, these consequences may be positive, as when teasing demonstrates camaraderie or when complaining is used as an icebreaker to make conversation flow more easily. Some couples even report that their relationships are stronger after they have survived a betrayal than they were before. Most of the time, however, the consequences for relationships are negative. Repeated annoyances among friends, intimate partners, and family members can lead to avoidance, mistrust, termination of the relationship, and violence. In addition, negative consequences may spill over into other close relationships. If a relationship ends because one partner has betrayed the other, for example, the mistrust engendered by the betrayal may be carried over into subsequent relationships, so that the victim is overly watchful for any signs of betrayal by a new partner. Similarly, a history of malicious teasing in your family may lead you to be overly sensitive to teasing in your adult relationships with friends and romantic partners.

Ultimately, the consequences for relationships depend on how the individuals involved work through the hurtful exchanges. People will always complain and people will always tell little white lies. Some people are by nature more likely to be dependent and clingy than others. People will always engage in indecorous, rude, and obnoxious behaviors. You cannot avoid them. How you choose to respond to them and whether the perpetrator makes an effort to stop them determine their ultimate impact on the relationship. People who consistently respond with anger, bear grudges, or seek revenge will generally experience more negative consequences in their relationships than people who try to understand the behavior and work to help the perpetrator modify it. Similarly, perpetrators who are insensitive to or ignore the effects of their behavior on others and continue to behave in ways they know their partners find annoying will experience more negative consequences than people who show that they are making at least some effort to stop the behaviors. This is not to say that victims should just put up with troublesome behavior to maintain a relationship. Indeed, such a passive response could be just as harmful to the relationship as anger.

Given the inevitability of annoying behaviors, it is unrealistic to expect that they will not occur or will have no negative consequences. As John Gottman (1994) has noted, however, as long as our positive exchanges with the people close to us exceed the negative ones by a ratio of at least 5 to 1, we should experience satisfaction in those relationships.

CONSEQUENCES TO THE INDIVIDUAL

The cumulative effect of annoying behaviors over time can be harmful to the individuals involved. A glance back at some of the reasons that these behaviors are troubling suggests why. When we perceive that our friend or romantic partner no longer values our relationship as much as we do, the hurt we feel can cut to the core of who we are. Unsure why we are no longer valued as much as we were or would like to be, we may think there is something wrong with us. When we tell ourselves that something about us must have led the person we care for to lie to us or reject us or put us down, our self-esteem plummets.

Our self-esteem may also be affected by the embarrassment and humiliation we may feel in response to some of the behaviors. Adolescent boys in the locker room whose peers tease them about the size of their genitals will be embarrassed and perhaps become self-conscious about their bodies. The loss of face that accompanies such behaviors is often difficult for some people to restore. In the course of my research on teasing, I have been amazed by the negative effects that long-ago teasing still has on people. One of my subjects said, "It was the first time I had been teased about my appearance. I will never forget how low it made me feel about myself." Another said, "It was the most unforgettable experience of my life." Another: "Such incidents leave permanent scars and are never really forgotten."

By contrast, the self-esteem of people who perpetrate annoying behaviors is often raised, at least temporarily. One of my respondents who years earlier had joined in bullying another little boy wrote, "We were absurd and childish, but because of our own insecurities—insecurities that I think almost every child experiences at that age—we gained strength and self-esteem from taking advantage of a helpless individual." People who behave arrogantly gain some gratification from making themselves appear better than anyone else. Finally, people who can control the feelings and behaviors of other people by lying to or about them and by complaining to them gain a sense of empowerment that can enhance their self-esteem, even if only for a short time.

Thus the behaviors we find troublesome in others and those that other people find troublesome in us may not be mere transitory annoyances. They may have long-lasting consequences not only for our current relationships but for those we seek to establish in the future; not only for the way we feel about ourselves at the moment but for the self-esteem (or lack of it) that we carry through life. They may be trivial, but all too often they are not.

2

• • • • • • • •

Complaining

Chronic complainers are never at a loss for something to complain about. Listen to Leslie:

> I am writing to complain about the fact that I am a chronic complainer. I never seem completely, 100 percent satisfied about anything. I complain about everything under the sun and I don't like to be like that. . . . Actually, I think I complain because that's how my mother is and it's just learned behavior. She is constantly critical and complaining about everything. She will criticize an overweight person, but she is overweight also. Or she'll complain about the large American flag on the pole in front of a restaurant located near the retirement apartment complex she lives in and says it's too big for the pole. . . . I work in an office and a coworker . . . is a complainer too. When we tell each other our complaints, we seem to laugh a lot because we're surprised to find someone else that feels like we do. But it seems that what we're doing is releasing the floodgates. Unfortunately, the rushing waters of complaints don't seem to be subsiding.

Everyone expresses dissatisfaction occasionally. We complain about ourselves ("I'm too lazy"), other people ("Boy, she's fat"), or the environment ("It's too hot to cook"). We whine, gripe, vent, kvetch, and even whinge (as they say in Australia) about nearly everything. Of all the annoying behaviors we are subjected to, complaining is one of the most common.

To appreciate how common complaining is, just listen to your own conversations. If you haven't complained about something yourself, someone else has. Complaining is so popular that Web sites are provided for "cyberventing" (McCafferty, 1999). The National Consumers League site (www.nclnet.org) receives as many as a thousand complaints every month. The Federal Trade Commission, responsible for consumer protection, receives 4,800 complaints monthly. Some online services mediate between complainers and corporations—for a fee, of course. If you log on to www.complaintbook.com, you can file a complaint about anything. Your complaint will be forwarded to the appropriate company or individual; if ComplaintBook receives a response, it, too, will be posted on the Web site. Of the complaints posted with ComplaintBook, 25 percent are directed against private organizations and 20 percent against government agencies; 24 percent are sent to providers of services, such as telephone companies. Interestingly, 5 percent of the complaints are directed at "no one in particular."

If you want to complain about complaining, a Web site is available to you, too. The Whiners of America (www.nowhining.com) sells "no whining" novelty and gift items. Even though we all tire of hearing complaints and there are times when a no whining T-shirt seems like just what we need, the frequency with which we all complain suggests that complaining is a topic worthy of investigation. Yet little research attention has been devoted to it.

The prevalence of complaining in our society today raises two questions. First, have people always complained as much as they do now? Second, does the frequency of complaining vary among regions of the world? Are people in the United States more likely to express dissatisfaction than people in other countries?

Although I have no definitive answer to either question, I can speculate with some confidence. People today, particularly those in Western cultures, do in fact seem to complain more than they once did. The primary reason is that our expectations have changed. When we are dissatisfied with a product, service, or person today, we are much more likely to gripe about it than people were thirty or forty years ago because we expect that something will be done to satisfy us. Our federal and state governments have issued regulations that tell us we deserve to have our grievances satisfied. Many choices and opportunities available to us today were unheard of a few decades ago. We have come to depend on the new technology, and we become frustrated when things don't work the way we expect. So when things don't go our way, our expectations are disconfirmed, we become dissatisfied, and we complain. If your internet service happens to be busy or down when you want to access your e-mail, how much time passes before you phone the customer service number to complain? Ten years ago, people would have been amazed at the possibility of having e-mail at all.

Readiness to complain, however, does not appear to be universal. People who seem to have the most to complain about—for example, a peasant planting corn in worn-out soil on a mountainside in Guatemala or a woman displaying her cucumbers in a village market in Romania—appear to complain the least. They have never had reason to expect much. They are well aware that many people are much better off than they are, but those people seem to be a different breed. These poor are much less likely than people in Western societies to compare themselves with others who are much more affluent than they are. A New York lawyer with an income of $250,000 a year envies the junior partner in a Wall Street law firm who pulls down $750,000, who in turn feels disadvantaged in comparison with the senior partners with their $2 million plus bonus. This phenomenon—social psychologists refer to it as relative deprivation (Collins, 1996)—would seem laughable to the poor of the third world. These people don't necessarily expect to have three meals a day or to have products that are always in working order—or any products at all. Expecting little or nothing, they do not complain.

Defining Complaining

Complaining is an expression of dissatisfaction. That much is obvious—but it's not the whole story. An expression of dissatisfaction does not necessarily mean that the complainer is actually dissatisfied; it may be a strategy employed to achieve some desired goal. A person may complain that he doesn't feel well when in fact he feels fine to avoid going to work. Inasmuch as people express dissatisfaction both when they are dissatisfied and when they are not, I have defined complaining as "an expression of dissatisfaction, whether subjectively experienced or not, for the purpose of venting emotions or achieving intrapsychic goals, interpersonal goals, or both" (Kowalski, 1996: 180).

Why Do People Complain?

In truth, the reasons people complain are as diverse as the complaints they express. Among the many functions that complaining serves, five are easily recognized: venting feelings (catharsis), lubricating social interactions, conveying a social image, comparing ourselves with others, and seeking explanations.

VENTING FEELINGS

Perhaps the most common function that complaining serves is venting our feelings, getting our frustrations off our chests. Think of all the cathartic complaining you do in your car as you express your outrage at other people's driving. Because the other drivers presumably can't hear your griping, your complaints will have no effect on their driving, but typically you feel better for having expressed them. One reason is that cathartic complaining stems from genuine feelings of dissatisfaction. The expression of dissatisfaction provides a release for hostile feelings. Terry recognized the value of cathartic complaining:

> Last semester I had a very boring professor. I could not stay focused in that class. Everybody else in the class felt the same way. On one of our tests, there was an opinion question, and when I got the test back, I found that my opinion question was graded wrong. I really thought that wasn't right. I have a right to my opinion, don't I? I complained to other people in the class. It really made me feel better to complain to the other class members.

The benefits of cathartic complaining are obvious when we examine what happens to people who don't vent their dissatisfaction by complaining. Think about a time when you were extremely unhappy with someone else's behavior but for whatever reason held back from saying anything about it. The more you inhibited any expression of dissatisfaction, the more it weighed on your mind and the angrier you became. When you finally did complain, you probably exploded in a way out of all proportion to the offense.

Making mountains out of molehills is only one of the problems suffered by people who inhibit expression of their emotions. These people may lay themselves open to the consequences of a Type C or Type D personality style, both characterized by the inhibition of emotional expression. The Type C personality is the cancer-prone personality. People with a Type C personality are perceived as very nice because they seldom complain and try to avoid conflict (Holland and Lewis, 1996). The result, however, is a decline in the functioning of the immune system, which increases the likelihood of physical health problems. People with a Type D personality are at increased risk for coronary artery disease

(Denollet, 1991; Denollet et al., 1996). The hormones that are released in response to the stress of inhibiting emotional expression have negative effects on the coronary artery system. People who seldom complain are also at increased risk for depression (Folkman and Lazarus, 1986). Failure to complain is no indication that such people are quite satisfied. Indeed, they may be very dissatisfied. Ruminating about their dissatisfaction until it assumes gigantic proportions can easily lead to depression. This association between rumination and depression appears to be a particular problem for women, who are more likely than men to inhibit expressions of negative feelings and thus to be prey to depression (Jack, 1991).

In addition, people who keep silent may find other, less adaptive outlets for the expression of their dissatisfaction. A prison inmate offered the following insight into just such an outcome:

> I've always noticed that complaining in a prison setting caused big problems. If the guys kept in their complaints, they tended to end up in mental health wards. If they were too vocal in complaining, they ended up on lockup. Therefore, there is no legitimate outlet for complaints in this deviate, closed society. Not counselors, preachers, guards, etc. If you complain to fellow prisoners, they brand you as a weakling or a sissy. Not a stand-up man. If a prisoner complains about any perceived situation to the outside (a media person, say), he's told, "Stop your whining, you were sent to prison to be punished." So . . . I can see why the return rate to prison is so high. Instead of voicing any complaints, they would tend to act out this suppressed rage when they're released.

Thus complaining would seem to be very beneficial for a person's emotional and psychological health. Too much cathartic complaining, however, may have negative consequences that offset its positive effects. People who complain too much come to be known as bores. We tire of their endless whining and eventually withdraw from them. In light of the potential drawbacks of cathartic complaining, the take-home message is that it should be used in moderation.

LUBRICATING SOCIAL INTERACTIONS

Like many other annoying behaviors, complaining can be used constructively as a social lubricant. Particularly when we're required to mingle with people we don't know, we often feel uncomfortable and socially anxious. Think back to a time when you were sitting in a waiting room next to strangers. You were probably unsure whether you should talk to them, smile at them, or simply ignore them. If you decided to talk to them, what did you say? One thing you might have chosen to do is to complain about something, such as the temperature in the room or the long wait ahead for all of you. Used in this way, complaining serves as an icebreaker; it allows people to start conversations that might otherwise be difficult. Even a lull in a conversation between friends can be eased by a mild complaint.

CONVEYING A SOCIAL IMAGE

All of us attempt to control the impressions that others form of us. These efforts are what psychologists are referring to when they speak of "self-presentation" or "impression management" (Leary, 1995; Leary and Kowalski, 1990). People who make favorable impressions will be liked and accepted; those who make unfavorable impressions risk being rejected and excluded. Thus people sometimes do certain things and refrain from doing others in efforts to control the ways other people see them.

Complaints can be used in a variety of ways to control other people's impressions of us (Kowalski, 1996). An expression of dissatisfaction with a service, for example, implies that the service is not up to your standards or expectations. Unless the service really is exceptionally poor, your complaint conveys the impression that your standards or expectations must be high. You may complain about the food or wine at a restaurant to show others that you are discriminating in your tastes. Perhaps even more commonly, you may complain about your health or your fatigue to excuse a performance that you fear may not be up to snuff. If I am concerned that I may not play well in a tennis match against you, I may preemptively complain about soreness in my ankle. Then if I lose the tennis game, everyone can attribute the loss to the sore ankle. And if I win the game in spite of the sore ankle, I must be an exceptional player.

The same concerns about self-presentation that lead us to complain can sometimes inhibit complaints. Nobody has a very high opinion of chronic complainers; we call them whiners and gripers, and we try to avoid them. To avoid being considered a whiner, we may stifle our complaints, or at the very least save them for someone who can be expected to listen without rejecting us.

Paradoxical as it may seem, concern about our image may also lead us to complain about something that makes us happy. Imagine that you and your best friend have applied to the same colleges and that both of you have put the same college at the top of your lists. The college of your choice accepts you but rejects your best friend. How do you handle your excitement and joy without making your friend feel even worse? One way is to complain. If you complain about how difficult the school will be, how far away from home it is, or how costly it will be to go there, you will still be talking about having gotten into the school you both wanted but in a way that will not antagonize your friend.

COMPARING OURSELVES WITH OTHERS

We all compare ourselves with others. When we seek other people's opinions, we generally do so to find out where we stand in comparison with them. Complaining is one way of finding out. If you've taken a test that you found very difficult, for instance, you'll probably wonder how others thought they did on the test. One way to get this information is to express dissatisfaction with the test: "That test was so hard!" or "That stuff about Pavlov—we didn't cover all that in class." Presumably your classmates will respond with their own views of the test: "Oh, yeah, I thought it was incredibly hard." By complaining about the test, you have elicited information that allows you to assess whether your feelings about the test are similar to or different from those of other students. If you find that other students share your feelings about the test, you will probably be less concerned about your performance than you would be if you found that everyone else thought it was easy. Thus complaining allows us to compare ourselves with others so that we can gain information that will help us evaluate our own performance.

SEEKING EXPLANATIONS

Within close relationships, many complaints are expressed to call others to account for their behavior. "You're always late getting home!"; "You never take the trash out when you say you will!" Often such complaints are typically expressed in the form of a question to indicate that a response is expected: "Why are you always late getting home?"; "Why do you never take the trash out when you say you will?" The complainant makes her dissatisfaction known while at the same time seeking an answer that will indicate a determination to do better.

What Do People Complain About?

People may complain about virtually anything. When you examine your own and other people's complaints, however, you realize that most of the things people complain about are trivial. There are three reasons why this is likely to be the case. First, rather than complain about major life events that cause us stress, people try to take constructive steps to eliminate the distress produced by such stressful events. Second, in the face of persistent life stress, learned helplessness sets in, a feeling that any effort to improve the situation is useless, and people simply don't feel like complaining. Third, it is possible that most people's complaints are trivial because the vast majority of their thinking is on trivial matters and on things that are concrete and more likely to have a direct effect on them. Thus, you may complain little about world hunger because you rarely think about it. But you frequently complain about the traffic because it is concrete and has a direct effect on you.

Partly because complaints tend to focus on trivial things, people typically express dissatisfaction with specific annoyances ("I hate it when he doesn't put the toilet seat down"), colloquially referred to as pet peeves, rather than more general complaints ("I'm miserable in this relationship"). When people are called upon to think about all of their pet peeves, they seem to have no difficulty generating a list. Indeed, a search of the World Wide Web for "pet peeve" yields more than 5,000 sites. Most of these Web sites are personal pages where people have simply listed their pet peeves. One such site is headed "Professors' Pet Peeves: How to Receive a Less than Enthusiastic Letter of Recommendation." Still others list pet peeves by category: "Miss America Contestant Pet Peeves," "Department Store Santa Pet Peeves," "Top 10 Indy 500 Driver Pet Peeves," "IRS Agent Pet Peeves." Most sites list pages and pages of pet peeves. At www.kvetch.com you can complain in real time with other kvetchers.

The *Atlanta Journal and Constitution* publishes a daily column titled "Vent" for people to voice their gripes. The *Waynesville* (North Carolina) *Mountaineer* similarly has a column titled "Pet Peeve of the Week." Among the pet peeves expressed by Waynesville readers: "Bad customer service. It only takes a moment to be polite. Just because you're having a bad day doesn't mean you should take it out on everyone else"; "People who let their dogs use the bathroom on the sidewalk and don't clean it up"; "People who don't turn right on red. After making a stop and checking traffic you can proceed right on red unless there is a sign saying otherwise. Pay attention please." Louie Hulme (1994) has published a small book titled *Pet Peeves: More than 200 Irritations from Everyday Life*. Ironically, one of his pet peeves is people who complain too much.

Clearly, then, pet peeves are a common part of people's lives, a part that they feel the need to voice. Even Dave Barry (1996) has devoted a column to pet peeves. Barry took issue with riders who rev their Harleys while simply sitting in a parking spot, able-bodied drivers who park in handicapped spots, and people who always send their food back, turning, as he says, "every single meal into an exercise in consumer whining."

Because my students and I were interested in the actual content of people's pet peeves and because most people's pet peeves arise in the context of relationships with friends and family members, we conducted a study of pet peeves in close relationships. Participants in the study were reminded that people involved in romantic relationships often develop pet peeves or irritations with things that their partner says or does. They were then asked to list as many pet peeves as they could think of with respect to their current or a former relationship partner.

We placed the pet peeves in categories: health, social behavior, personality, hygiene, manners, disrespect, unconscious annoyances, communication, idiosyncrasies, relational issues, family issues, acting out in public. Table 2.1 shows some of the pet peeves. Here we see that the pet peeves expressed—the full number was staggering—range from the mundane to the serious.

Men expressed significantly fewer pet peeves than women. The discrepancy became even more pronounced when we examined

Table 2.1. Pet Peeves

Health	*Manners*
Working out every day	Rudeness
Smoking	Eating too loudly
Drinking	Slobbering when kissing
Not wearing seat belt	Spitting
	Chewing with mouth open
Social behavior	Talking through a movie
Acting differently around friends	Disrespect
Bringing up embarrassing things	One person always paying for stuff
Flirtatious with other people	Slapping butt
Always comparing	Teasing and joking
Talking differently when others in room	Prejudiced statements
Forwarding e-mails	Borrowing things
	Pressure to do something
Personality	Snooping through accounts
Defensiveness	Lateness
Control freak	Selfishness
Girls acting blondish	Tilting shower head
Indecisiveness	Always picking channels
Moodiness	Lying
Irresponsibility	Treating cats roughly
Rocking	Being told what to do
Neatness	Drinking beer when we don't have much left
Stuck on himself	Taking lots of time
Her attitude	
Fairy tale world	*Unconscious annoyances (forgetfulness)*
Pouting	
Always has to be talking	Not replacing toilet paper roll
	Twirling hair until it knots
Hygiene	Tags out of shirt
Not shaving legs	Smacking lips while chewing gum
Picking nose	Snoring
Squirting toothpaste in mouth	Biting nails
Sleep in eyes	Grabbing himself
Washing hair with cup	Jiggling legs
Leaving stuff in refrigerator	Spasmodic clapping

Table 2.1. Pet Peeves (continued)

Always looking at watch	*Relational issues*
Letting alarm clock go off	Does not speak
Communication	Spending hours on computer
Talking too fast	Never calling
Not telling me what's annoying him	Lack of trust
Repeating things	Bringing up past relationships
Not asking directions	Wanting affection in public
Nicknames	Always says I've changed
Yelling	Wanting to know if we'll get married
Complaining/nagging	Needing personal space
Saying one thing and doing another	Double standard
Talking jargon	Wanting sex three times a day
Asking about something I already told him	Jealousy
Saying "like"	Irrational guilt trips
	Bringing up past
Idiosyncrasies	Tries to be my mom
Phone being busy all the time	Breaking up, then wanting to get back together
Not keeping up with current events	
Shoes and belt don't match	*Family issues*
Mayo with fries	Letting mother run his life
Personal preferences	Calling his mother
Dog under table	
"I did it because I had no choice"	*Acting out in public*
Always moving when mad	Singing
	Dancing

the number of pet peeves that fell within each category. In all categories women expressed almost twice as many pet peeves as men and in some, such as disrespect and unconscious annoyances, four times as many. We might suspect that women are more willing to voice their dissatisfaction or that men have a tendency to behave in ways that annoy women, but we don't believe either of those explanations. We believe rather that women are more sensitive than men to other people's behaviors. Because women are more oriented to relationships than men are, they are more likely to pick up on both positive and negative features of those relationships. (Do I hear you mutter that that's a stereotype? If there were no truth to stereotypes, they couldn't get to be stereotypes.) The same quality that attunes women to subtle nuances in others' behavior makes them alert to the bothersome aspects of that behavior.

Who Complains?

Everyone complains at least occasionally, so we must distinguish between complaining and being a complainer. Although most people complain about some aspect of their lives several times a day, most people are not called complainers. Complainers complain regularly regardless of whom they are with or what the circumstances. A complainer either is truly dissatisfied with everything and everyone or at least wants everyone else to think so.

Some years ago I was interested in determining who the complainers are. To identify differences in the frequency with which people complain, I generated the Complaining Propensity Scale, consisting of fourteen items (table 2.2). When you have completed the scale, following the directions provided, score the items marked "(R)" in reverse. In other words, change a 5 to 1, a 4 to 2, a 2 to 4, and a 1 to 5; 3 remains 3. Once you have made these changes, add up your scores.

Your complaining propensity score is meaningless by itself. It becomes meaningful when we discover that roughly 50 percent of people score below 45 and 50 percent score above 45. If your score falls below 45, then, you may consider yourself an infrequent complainer. If your score is above 45, you fall into the range of chronic complainers. Clearly, the higher you score above 45, the more chronic a complainer you are likely to be.

Table 2.2. Complaining Propensity Scale

Indicate how characteristic of you each of the items below is, using the following scale:

1 = Not at all characteristic of me
2 = Somewhat characteristic of me
3 = Moderately characteristic of me
4 = Very characteristic of me
5 = Extremely characteristic of me

_____ 1. Whenever I am dissatisfied, I readily express it to other people.
_____ 2. I frequently express dissatisfaction with the behavior of others.
_____ 3. I don't usually vent my frustrations or dissatisfactions. (R)
_____ 4. When people annoy me, I tell them.
_____ 5. I seldom inform others that I am disappointed. (R)
_____ 6. I usually keep my discontent a secret. (R)
_____ 7. When someone does something to make me feel bad, I am likely to inform that person of my displeasure.
_____ 8. I tend to complain a great deal.
_____ 9. I seldom state my dissatisfaction with the behavior of others. (R)
_____ 10. I generally don't say much when I am dissatisfied. (R)
_____ 11. I usually vent my dissatisfaction.
_____ 12. I keep my dissatisfactions to myself.
_____ 13. When I am unhappy or upset, I usually keep it to myself. (R)
_____ 14. When people or events don't meet my expectations, I usually communicate my dissatisfaction.

One might expect the scores of men and women on the Complaining Propensity Scale to differ. Stereotypes, as well as the results of our own pet peeve study, would lead us to believe that women complain more than men. Yet men and women do not appear to differ in the frequency with which they complain; the difference lies in their views of complaining. What men view as complaining, women are more likely to perceive as confiding. Thus what appear to be differences in the frequency of men's and women's complaining are in fact differences in the ways they interpret complaints.

Help-Rejecting Complainers

A small subset of chronic complainers, the help-rejecting complainers (Frank et al., 1952), are the most difficult of all to deal with (Kowalski and Erickson, 1997). These people complain to seek help and advice, then reject all the help and advice that are offered (Yalom, 1985). Eric Berne, in his book *Games People Play* (1964), described these people as playing the "Why don't you ... Yes but" game. The game goes like this: One person asks another for advice about a problem; the other person offers suggestions that typically take the form of "Why don't you ..." No matter what suggestions are offered, the advice seeker responds with "Yes but ..."

Help-rejecting complainers tend to exaggerate the magnitude of their problems. They feel that their problems merit more attention than anyone else's, and because they see no hope of finding a satisfactory solution, they make no effort to alleviate the problem. Their passivity stems from three sources: it is unlikely that any solution offered to them has not already occurred to them; even if a new recommendation is made, they consider it hopeless; and they may not actually be looking for a solution, but simply want to complain.

Many people repeatedly seek advice, support, reassurance, and attention. What differentiates the help-rejecting complainer from people who are simply overeager for reassurance is their consistent rejection of the help they are offered. Indeed, it is this characteristic, even more than the relentlessness of their complaining, that makes help-rejecting complainers so bothersome.

To Whom Do We Complain?

The audience you choose for your complaints depends on whether you are an effective or an ineffective complainer. Effective complainers are selective. When they want to change something that bothers them, they complain to people who are most likely to listen and to help them deal constructively with their dissatisfaction.

Ineffective complainers complain to anyone who will lend them even half an ear. It's sometimes unclear whether they really want a solution or simply want to complain. Many of those who really do want to be heard seek out a professional therapist to whom they can complain nonstop for fifty minutes at a time.

Barbara Held addresses the distinction between ineffective complainers and effective ones, or what she calls "creative kvetchers," in *Stop Smiling, Start Kvetching* (1999). According to Held, a creative kvetcher is not just someone who complains on and on to anyone within earshot. Rather, a creative kvetcher is sensitive to the listener's "kvetch reception potential (KRP)," or ability to listen to others' complaints. A person with a low KRP will make a poor listener. After all, as Eeyore says in *Eeyore's Gloomy Little Instruction Book* (Powers, 1996), "It's bad enough being miserable, but it is even worse when everyone else claims to be miserable, too."

For creative kvetchers who at the moment are unable to find anyone with a high KRP, such avenues as letters to the editor allow them to vent their feelings without risking disapproval and rejection. In an examination of complaining in the media, my students and I reviewed the content of 166 letters to the editors of newspapers throughout the country (Mathews-Coleman et al., 1997). The greatest percentage of these letters reflected global complaints about people, objects, and events. Next came complaints reflecting a desire for change. Every letter to the editor that we read contained at least one complaint; one contained fifteen. The average number was just over three.

We found geographical differences in the number of complaints the letter writers expressed. People living in the Southeast and Northwest expressed significantly fewer complaints in their submissions to regional newspapers than people whose letters were published in such national newspapers as *USA Today* and the *Wall Street Journal*. These differences may be a function of the selection criteria used by the editors of national papers, the writers of the letters, the nature of the newspapers, or social norms regarding complaining in different parts of the country.

What Makes Complaining Annoying?

Few of us are annoyed by occasional expressions of dissatisfaction. How could we be, when we complain regularly ourselves? In view of the frequency with which we all complain and listen to others complain, complaining could not be entirely annoying. Four factors seem to distinguish complaints that are annoying from those that are not: their repetitiveness, their content, their instrumentality, and their intentionality (Kowalski and Erickson, 1997).

UNENDING COMPLAINING

The complaining that is perhaps most obnoxious is the kind that never ends. People who occasionally express dissatisfaction are rarely viewed as annoying. In fact, we may welcome a little complaining as a means of getting to know the complainers and the way they feel about things. But we generally try to avoid people who go on and on and on about their dissatisfaction with everything. One reason is that when people complain to anyone about everything, their complaining does not appear to be genuine. Incessant complainers not only are tiresome, they have a credibility problem. Another reason for our annoyance is that incessant complainers are clearly not taking the listener into consideration. We all have our problems. We're usually glad to commiserate with a person who has a genuine complaint, but to ask us to listen to a chronicle of woes that never ends is to ask too much.

ANNOYING CONTENT OF COMPLAINTS

The content of some complaints is far more annoying than that of others. That is not news to anyone who has raised a child. As Leslie Boyd (1997) has pointed out, "the greedy whine" is heard most frequently as parents stand with their little darlings in the checkout line at the supermarket, next to those enticing displays of candy and gum. This type of whine, Boyd recommends, should be ignored. The "yawning whine" reflects simple fatigue and should be attended to: put the child to bed as soon as possible. Parents' responses to these whines differ because the first is more annoying than the second.

But what is it about the content of some adults' complaints that makes them so annoying? I have pinpointed three things: the authenticity of the complaint, its verifiability, and its directness (Kowalski and Erickson, 1997). Some complaints are authentic in the sense that they stem from genuine feelings of dissatisfaction, whereas other complaints are motivated not by true dissatisfaction but by a belief that complaining will allow the complainer to achieve some other goal. If I am truly sick and complain that I don't feel well, I am expressing an authentic complaint. But if I complain about not feeling well when in fact I feel fine, my complaint is not authentic. Similarly, if I insist that last night's indigestion was a heart attack, I have also expressed an inauthentic complaint. Although inauthentic complaints are not inherently obnoxious (after all, who will know if I am really sick or not?), most people are much less tolerant when they sense that an expression of dissatisfaction is not genuine.

Can the complaint be verified—supported by objective evidence? If you complain about a hole in a coat that you just retrieved from the cleaners, your complaint is verifiable because you have clear evidence to back it up. A nonverifiable complaint reflects a personal opinion that cannot be substantiated. If you repeatedly complain about the music played on the local radio station, your complaint cannot be verified; it reflects only your personal opinion, nothing more. Because nonverifiable complaints are subjective, listeners tend to be much less tolerant of them than of complaints that can be verified.

How direct is the complaint? If you are dissatisfied with the way your microwave oven performs, have you addressed your complaint directly to the company that is responsible for your dissatisfaction? Or have you complained only to friends and neighbors who are willing to listen? The Federal Trade Commission estimates that people in the United States are unhappy with 75 million purchases annually, but only 4 percent of consumers ever issue a formal complaint (Robinson, 1997).

The directness or indirectness of a complaint has fewer implications when the dissatisfaction is caused by a consumer product than when it is caused by an individual. Although a complaint expressed directly to the person with whom you are dissatisfied can produce distress and defensiveness, it can be quite effective in changing the behavior you object to. If you complain indirectly to a third party, however, you'll succeed only in damaging the relationship between at least two people: the person who aroused your complaint is unlikely to change his behavior because he is not aware that you object to it; and since you are unlikely to complain about him to someone who does not know him, you have set the scene for some potentially awkward interactions in the future between the two of them.

INSTRUMENTALITY OF COMPLAINTS

Most consumer complaints are instrumental: they are expressed in an effort to bring about some change. For that matter, most direct complaints are instrumental, aimed at changing the source of annoyance. Noninstrumental or expressive complaints are those that are expressed for their cathartic value. If I vehemently complain that the sneakers I bought yesterday for $89 and am wearing even as I speak are on sale for $59 today, I won't get a refund, but I may feel better for having vented my frustration.

Although both instrumental and expressive complaints have benefits, particularly for the complainer, listeners tend to be more accepting of instrumental complaints than of expressive ones. People who repeatedly complain but never take any practical steps to decrease their dissatisfaction become tiresome.

INTENTIONALITY OF COMPLAINTS

The vast majority of complaints are mindless. In fact, most people are unaware of how often they complain and would be embarrassed if it were pointed out to them. Not all complaints are mindless, however; some are meant to change someone's behavior or to manipulate another person. Because few of us like to have our behavior called into question, we tend to be defensive in the face of complaints we perceive to be intentional or manipulative.

In the long run, though, mindless complaining is of less interpersonal benefit than intentional complaining. Mindless complaining accomplishes nothing but making the complainer feel better. Intentional complaining, however, because it is motivated by a desire to put an end to someone else's annoying behavior, may ultimately improve the quality of a relationship. If I am repeatedly annoyed by my partner's continued failure to take out the trash, I may complain repeatedly in the hope of changing his behavior. Should he in fact begin to carry out the trash regularly, then my mood improves, the nagging stops, and the quality of the relationship improves.

Consequences of Complaining

The fact that some complaints are more annoying than others implies that the consequences of complaints will also vary. On the

positive side, complaining can be beneficial personally, relation-
ally, and materially. Given the frequency with which people complain, there is obviously some personal benefit to be had, primarily
in the form of improved mood. As Jasper Griegson (1998) suggests, simply the act of doing something about one's dissatisfaction is enough to make one feel better. Research does show that
immediately after complaining, people feel worse (Kowalski and
Cantrell, 2002), but this finding might have been expected: after
all, in order to complain, one must think about one's dissatisfaction. The complainer's mood improves quickly, however, and the
affective benefits of complaining become clear.

   Complaining that puts an end to annoying behavior can improve relationships. Similarly, complaining to companies about
poor service can result in credits, exchanges of products, or cou-
pons for services to be redeemed later. An article in the *Waynesville
Mountaineer* (August 25, 1999) was headed "Complaints Can Pay,
Cable Customer Finds." The customer's repeated complaints to
the cable company about his poor reception of several cable chan-
nels resulted in credits to his cable bill. A woman who claimed
that she regularly sent letters of complaint to companies that provide poor service reported that she had received free airline tickets,
hotel rooms, and meals (Robinson, 1997). There are even books
on the lucrativeness of complaining. Griegson's *Joys of Complaining* (1998) is billed as "the complainer's guide to getting even
more." The consensus is that to be effective, a letter of complaint
should always be addressed to the head of the company, should
be brief and to the point, and should state specifically what the
complainant wants and set a deadline for the resolution of the
complaint.

   The consequences of complaining can also be negative for complainers but perhaps even more so for listeners. As E. C. Mc-
Kenzie (1980: 95) noted, "It's better to complain occasionally and
carry your own burdens than cheerfully push them off on some-

one else." The greatest risk for complainers is rejection when others tire of hearing the complaints. The risk to listeners is that they will themselves become dissatisfied after listening to others' complaints, an effect I call mood contagion. Just as people who must spend much time with a depressed person often find that they begin to feel depressed themselves, so people who associate with frequent complainers report that they, too, begin to feel dissatisfied. If you complain to me about the annoyances of the latest version of Windows, I'll be reminded that I'm not too happy about it myself. In one of the Winnie-the-Pooh stories, Christopher Robin suggests that the residents of the Hundred Acre Wood are experiencing a bad case of the "Galloping Grumps." When Piglet asks if it's catching, Christopher Robin says, "Very catching. . . . Grumpiness and grouchiness gallop very quickly from one person to another" (Birney, 1992). Clearly implied is the likelihood that listeners who are reminded of their own dissatisfaction will themselves become complainers and will infect other people with grouchiness, in a domino effect.

These negative effects of complaining on the listener are made clear in a letter I received from a woman who had tired of listening to people complain:

> I am about to give up a job that pays more than any other I've had because I can't listen to the complaints any more. The position involves the management of a long-term health care unit, staffing, budgets, and marketing. This is a breeze compared to the complaints and negative comments I hear from the residents on an ongoing daily basis, only a very small proportion of which are valid. And when the valid concerns are resolved, it wasn't done fast enough, good enough, or the way it was done in the past. I've only held this position for three months but I give up.

But what about those people who seem to have limitless patience as they listen to others' complaints and who seem to suffer no adverse effects? Professional therapists listen to the complaints of their clients all day long. What allows them to hear their clients out without catching the Galloping Grumps? Or do they? Do some people make better complaint listeners than others?

In an attempt to answer this question, Mark Brendle and I examined the job satisfaction and personality characteristics of hospital patient representatives, also known as complaint representatives, because their primary task is to listen to patients' complaints. As a whole, the patient representatives indicated that patients' complaints had no particular effect on their own feelings. Only 15 percent of those surveyed said they had ever thought about leaving their jobs. The reasons they gave for their dissatisfaction included inability to leave the pressures of work behind at the end of the day and feeling that they were not a positive influence on their patients. Dissatisfied individuals were also more likely to report feeling emotionally drained, frustrated by their jobs, and unable to care about some patients; working with patients all day was a strain. The patient representatives who scored high on the Complaining Propensity Scale reported that they found their jobs emotionally draining.

What is notable about these results is the small percentage of people who found dissatisfaction in listening to others complain all day. This finding suggests that some people do indeed make better complaint listeners than others.

What to Do?

What can and should be done about complaining is really a two-fold question: What can each of us do to reduce our own complaining and how can we learn to deal better with people who chronically complain to us?

SOLUTIONS FOR THE COMPLAINER

How can you train yourself to stop complaining if you're not aware that you *are* complaining? The vocabulary of complaining is such a prominent part of our language that many constant complainers are truly unaware that they are complaining. Thus the first step toward limiting our own complaining is to increase our awareness of the frequency and content of our complaints. We simply have to monitor our style of interacting with others and note how often our interactions involve complaining.

Armed with the knowledge that some complaining is constructive, we are now ready for the next step in altering our complaining behavior: learning to discriminate constructive complaints from those that are unnecessary or actually destructive. Even constructive complaints, however, can be expressed in a way that grates on other people's nerves. So we must take care to express complaints in a tone that suggests a request or an expression of concern rather than a whine. Our last step is to increase our awareness of the effects of complaining on others. We would all be more effective complainers if we were better at picking up on cues that our audience is tired of hearing us complain, that they simply don't want to hear any more.

SOLUTIONS FOR THE LISTENER

For people who have to listen to others complain only occasionally, perhaps the best response is a simple acknowledgment. People who complain relatively infrequently often just want a little empathy or an acknowledgment that their complaints have some merit.

Dealing with chronic complainers, on the other hand, can be a problem. You might simply ignore the complainer or give very short responses. The problem here is that such responses often increase the chronic complainer's dissatisfaction, and the complaints escalate. If you take the other tack and respond with great interest, asking the chronic complainer to elaborate, you convey the impression that you are eager to listen and that the complainer can always find a ready ear—yours. Either way, the listener is in for more complaints.

In *Games People Play*, Berne suggests that one of the most effective ways to deal with people who play the "Why don't you . . . Yes but" game is to acknowledge that their complaints have been heard, but then to turn the tables and ask them what they plan to do about their dissatisfaction. This call for a response generally silences the complaints.

What you do when you're confronted with a chronic complainer will be affected by who the complainer is. Your response to an adult whiner, for instance, may differ from your response to a whining child. Many people view whining as a developmental stage that children go through between crying and making a verbal request. The problem is that when whining is ignored, it generally continues until it brings some response; and if the response is the one the child desires, the child may see no need to move on to the verbal request stage (Boyd, 1997). You can avoid that outcome by letting the child know that whining and complaining will always be ignored, but that asking in a pleasant, noncomplaining way will bring a response. The response may be no, but if it's delivered without anger or impatience, with a brief explanation, and with the promise of some alternative reward for the child's appropriate behavior, whining is unlikely to recur.

Such responses may be adapted for a whining adult. You can choose to ignore the whiner (yes, that's generally easier said than done) and you can respond to more appropriate behavior in a way that rewards it. If your relationship with the whiner is sufficiently solid, you may elect a more confrontational response, said, of course, with care and a little ironic humor: "It's time you quit

complaining and *did* something about it!" Perhaps the simple embarrassment of being called a complainer will end the complaining, at least for a while. Finally, we can set limits to the amount
of complaining we will listen to, and we can make those limits
known to the complainers. We can tell them explicitly that we're
happy to listen to them constructively express their dissatisfaction,
but we don't have the time or the inclination to listen to them
drone on and on, particularly when they're unable or unwilling to
do anything about the things that trouble them.

Complaining, then, can be a major annoyance, but there's no reason to vow never to do it again. Complaining can bring rewards
if we do it at the right time, in the right way, to the right person,
for the right reason. It can even be its own reward. Like all good
things, though, it can be overdone, and it usually is.

3

. . . .

Teasing and Bullying

Children chant, "Sticks and stones will break my bones but words will never hurt me"—but they know better. Lynn certainly did:

> I have never been proud of my physical appearance and I am extremely shy about my body. As I was growing up, I was always on the chubby side. When I was very young, I remember my family calling me Miss Piggy and Fatty and Blubberbutt. In school the boys never liked me. They used to talk about the "fat girl over there"—that would be me, standing somewhere alone. My mother used to carp at me about my weight. She was always telling me I needed to lose weight and even tried to bribe me. I felt like an embarrassment to her. . . . She used to compare my body with hers, how much skinnier she was than me. I lost forty pounds my freshman year at college, but I am still slightly over-weight. When I look in the mirror, I hate myself. I hate what I see. I can't even stand to let my fiancé see me naked.

The effects of teasing and bullying are seen in such books as *Lord of the Flies* and in such films as *My Bodyguard*. Countless newspaper and magazine articles tell of children who were bullied so relentlessly that they took their own lives. We know that words do hurt. As one student said, "Whoever said that sticks and stones will break my bones but words will never hurt me must have been deaf."

Can any of us claim that we have never been teased or have never teased anyone else? For all our bad memories of being targets of teasing, surely some memories of being teased bring a smile to our faces. The feelings we associate with teasing can be either positive or negative; the context is all. It's hard to see any positive effects of bullying. How is teasing related to bullying? At what point does innocent teasing become bullying? Although everyone has been exposed to teasing, not everyone can claim to have been bullied. Yet teasing is considered the most common type of bullying (Ross, 1996).

Defining Teasing and Bullying

Teasing and bullying have been very difficult to define. Think about all the meanings we attach to the word "tease" as a noun. When a woman removes her clothing piece by piece on the stage, her act is called a strip tease. A woman who leads men on but does not follow through with the sex act is called a tease. A second-string bull that is led to a cow to arouse her before the stud arrives is called a tease. A search of synonyms for "tease" as a verb also reveals a variety of interpretations: flirt, pester, coax, agitate, goad, harass, humiliate, kid, taunt, persecute, joke. Advertisers tease us with the illusion that their products will improve our health, beauty, and happiness. A middle-schooler teases another child about the shoes he is wearing.

Although "bully" has fewer meanings than "tease," it, too, is cloaked in ambiguity. What constitutes bullying? Is bullying the same as teasing? How long does a behavior have to persist before it qualifies as bullying? Is bullying always physical or can verbal abuse also be called bullying?

To lend some order to this confusion, I define teasing as "identity confrontation couched in humor" (Kowalski, Howerton, and McKenzie, 2001: 178). To tease is always to confront another person about some aspect of his identity. When my colleague teases me about wearing a brown corduroy jacket in April, she is confronting me about my taste or my parsimoniousness or my presumed poverty. By phrasing the confrontation as playful, a teaser can always say, "I was only kidding" when she realizes that perhaps the tease has embarrassed me.

Bullying, too, involves identity confrontation, but it may or may not be couched in humor. A bully who calls an overweight boy Lardass in no way conveys any intent to be funny. The bully appears to mean what he says. Because bullying is less likely than teasing to be humorous, it is generally less ambiguous. People may not know how to interpret a teaser's motives, but they rarely have any trouble seeing that a bully is trying to be mean.

Many people view teasing and bullying as the same thing. Indeed, students list teasing as the most frequent form of bullying. Although teasing and bullying are closely related, I do not agree that they are synonymous. Both consist of identity confrontation, humor, and ambiguity, but teasing and bullying can be distinguished by the ways these three elements are combined. When humor outweighs identity confrontation, we are dealing with teasing; when identity confrontation outweighs humor, we are dealing with bullying. This distinction also allows us to differentiate between good-natured and hurtful teasing. Good-natured teasing is high in humor, moderate in identity confrontation, and low to moderate in ambiguity; hurtful teasing is high in identity confrontation and moderate in both humor and ambiguity. Bullying is high in identity confrontation and low in humor and ambiguity. In addition, whereas teasing is usually a one-time thing, bullying generally continues over an extended period. Dan Olweus, the world's leading expert on bullying, considers that a child is being bullied when "he or she is exposed, repeatedly and over time, to negative actions on the part of one or more other students" (1993: 9). But consider a newspaper account of an incident in which three adolescent boys forced three younger boys playing in a sand-pit to undress and perform sexual acts on one another. They also poured sand on the boys and told them they would be buried alive ("Three boys assaulted," 1998). According to Olweus's definition, this episode could not be categorized as bullying. To my mind, however, even a single instance of such behavior constitutes bullying.

The Prevalence of Teasing and Bullying

In a survey of seven- and eleven-year-old children (Mooney, Cresser, and Blatchford, 1991), 96 percent of the children in each age group reported that teasing was common in their schools. Sixty-seven percent of the seven-year-olds and 57 percent of the eleven-year-olds also reported that they had been victimized by teasing. Fifty percent of the seven-year-olds and 57 percent of the eleven-year-olds admitted that they had teased other children. Statistics related to the prevalence of bullying closely mirror those of teasing. Over 90 percent of elementary and middle school children report bullying at their schools. That amounts to more than 5 million children who either are bullied or witness bullying at school. An estimated 160,000 school-aged children miss some school because they fear being bullied (*Asbury Park Press*, September 4, 1999, B1).

Although we know little about the actual frequency of teasing among adults, it is probably safe to say that the percentages of adults who tease and are teased mirror or exceed the percentages reported among children. The form that teasing takes, however, is likely to differ. Whereas children frequently tease by calling other children names, adults are more likely to tease about such things as people's sexual relationships (or lack thereof) or their weaknesses (a limp, a lack of athletic ability).

We know little about the prevalence of bullying among adults, either, but it seems likely that adults bully as frequently as children do, although the bullying may more readily be referred to as intimidation or domestic violence. Just as children use bullying to get other children to act a certain way or to hand over money or something else the bully wants, so adults use intimidation to get other people to go along with their wishes. Child bullies may physically beat their schoolmates to get them to comply; adult bullies may substitute verbal aggression or threatening body language, but do not always do so (Marano, 1998).

Changes in Teasing and Bullying Behavior with Age

Although we have some information about the frequency of teasing, we know little about how teasing and bullying change with age. At what age do children begin to tease? Does the nature of teasing remain constant across the life span? Is good-natured teasing more likely among younger children than older ones? Are younger children and older adults more likely than adolescents and young adults to favor positive teasing over the hurtful kind? Some of these questions are harder to answer than others. Determining the age at which children begin to tease, for example, has been difficult in large part because people disagree about whether a particular behavior by an infant or toddler is really teasing. Some researchers (Reddy, 1991) have suggested that children as young as nine months both tease and enjoy being teased: they will hold out a toy as if to hand it to another person, only to withdraw it as soon as someone reaches for it. Others, however, suggest that children do not begin to tease until they have developed more of a sense of themselves and their surroundings, beginning around the age of two years. In other words, children will not begin to tease until they understand that their behavior has an effect on other people: that they can make others laugh or respond to them. Regardless of the specific age at which teasing begins, teasing among young children is virtually always delightful.

Teasing does not remain charming forever, alas. By adolescence teasing frequently takes on a decidedly nasty tone. Because adolescents have more experience with language than preschoolers, they have become adept at framing their teases in ambiguous ways that the target can interpret either positively or negatively.

Researchers who investigated the differences in the teasing of younger and older children (Oswald et al., 1987) found that six-year-olds were as likely to tease children of the opposite sex as those of the same sex, and that the teasing of the opposite sex was no more likely to be mean. Whereas the targets of the six-year-olds generally perceived their teasing as playful, the targets of teasing by ten-year-olds often interpreted it as malicious. Among the ten-year-olds, girls were more bothered by teasing than boys.

Because bullying is more insidious, it typically begins later than teasing, usually among children who are entering kindergarten or first grade. This is not to say that bullying does not occur before about age five, only that children are less able to identify what is happening to them as bullying before that age. The number of children who report being victimized by bullies gradually declines as children progress through grade school and middle school, but the bullying episodes that do occur tend to be more intense and malicious than those that occurred in early childhood (Marano, 1998). The bullying episodes also tend to be directed repeatedly toward particular individuals rather than indiscriminately.

We know little about changes in teasing and bullying after adolescence. Although the trends in early and middle childhood suggest that teasing and bullying become more ambiguous and more negative in tone as people age, common sense tells me that at some point teasing begins to become less negative. Teasing by the elderly resembles that of young children in frequency and tone; typically it is more good-natured than teasing among younger adults. Perhaps the elderly, having already lost friends and family members, may be unwilling to risk hurting other people. They may also use teasing in a friendly way to seek out other people and establish relationships with them. But so far as I know, no data have been collected on teasing and bullying among the elderly.

Who Teases and Bullies?

It is safe to say that almost everyone occasionally teases other people. So rather than asking who teases, perhaps we should be asking who teases regularly or who is most likely to be a chronic teaser. What little attention has been paid to this issue has identified members of social groups rather than persons with identifiable characteristics. When researchers asked elementary and middle school children who teased the most, for example, the most common responses were aggressive bullies and popular children (Shapiro, Baumeister, and Kessler, 1991). Surely aggressive bullies are not popular, so how can it be that children who are popular tease as much as the bullies? It helps to notice that bullies and popular children have something else in common: both are dominant among their schoolmates. By teasing, members of both groups can display their superior position in relation to the other children. Furthermore, being dominant may provide people the freedom to be less concerned with what others think, so they may be less concerned with any negative consequences that may follow from teasing others.

We still know little about the personality characteristics of chronic teasers. We all know a chronic tease when we meet one, but what features of these persons really distinguish them as chronic teases? To find out, April Watts Brooks and I (1998) asked a group of people to list all the behaviors or characteristics they associate with a chronic tease. After we eliminated redundancies among the lists, a total of 125 behaviors and characteristics remained. We then had another group rate how characteristic each of these 125 behaviors and characteristics was of a chronic tease. The 20 behaviors and characteristics listed as most descriptive of a chronic tease are shown in table 3.1. An examination of these characteristics reveals why teasing has both positive and negative features. The same person who is described as a pain in the butt and manipulative, for instance, is also described as liking to joke and having a sense of humor.

Certain personality characteristics do seem to distinguish people who tease and bully frequently from those who don't. People who are polite and considerate are more likely to engage in good-natured teasing than people who are less considerate; people who are extroverted and outgoing tease others frequently, but those who are conscientious and agreeable do not (Georgesen et al., 1999).

Many people believe that bullies have low self-esteem—that putting others down is a way for them to feel better about themselves. It appears, however, that bullies have very favorable, if somewhat distorted, views of themselves. School-age bullies see themselves as liked far more than they actually are. Interestingly, despite their inability to determine their own status in the social hierarchy, bullies have no trouble determining just how well liked other children are (Marano, 1998). They are very adept at selecting the person low in the pecking order as a target for their bullying.

Our investigation into who teases would be incomplete if we failed to consider whether teasing is more characteristic of men or women, boys or girls. Although there is some disagreement here, the consensus appears to be that boys and men tease more than girls and women. More firm evidence suggests that boys

Table 3.1. Characteristics of Chronic Teasers

Acts rude and abusive toward others
Lacks self-confidence or self-esteem
Has a sense of humor
Wants to be accepted
A happy person who enjoys life
Loud
Annoys and irritates others
Verbally and/or physically aggressive
Seeks attention from others
Likes to joke
Makes fun of others by mocking them
Laughs and cuts up
Talkative
Often flirts with others
Has a laid-back or carefree personality
Gives others nicknames
Is a pain in the butt
Dumb
Bullies others
Finds faults in others

Source: Adapted from " 'You Are Such a Tease!':
Identifying and Describing the Chronic Teaser," by
A. Watts. Master's thesis, Western Carolina Univer-
sity. Copyright © 1998 by A. Watts.

bully more than girls. As a former student of mine has noted, boys are raised in a culture that views teasing as a means of toughening them up. Dan Kindlon and Michael Thompson (1999) make a similar case for the culture of cruelty confronted by boys, particularly as they pass through adolescence. Adolescent boys who do or say anything that makes them appear different are harshly ridiculed by their peers—put down, humiliated, shamed.

A comparison of teasing and bullying among adolescent boys and adolescent girls attests to some gender differences. Whereas boys tend to go for the jugular when they tease, insulting and putting down their targets, girls' teasing tends to be more subtle; they may exclude or ostracize someone from their peer group or gossip about her (Simmons, 2002). Boys appear to be less concerned than girls about humiliating and embarrassing their targets. Perhaps for this reason, boys tend to dish it out far better than they take it. Indeed, boys report enjoying teasing others but seldom report enjoying being teased.

Who Gets Teased?

People who are different in any way from the majority—for example, those who have unusual names, some physical or developmental disability, or a strong accent—tend to be teased more frequently than people who have no immediately observable idiosyncrasy. A student in one of my studies told of being teased when she was riding the school bus: "I was the only person on the bus who had brown skin and so other kids teased me about it. The people who were teasing me had never been around anyone who was not white." Another student told about a time when she had teased someone else: "I was walking down a sidewalk and this guy was walking toward me. He was handicapped and retarded and had a bad leg. As soon as he passed, I started laughing and calling him names."

Yet people with the most distinguishing disability tend not to be teased as often as those with a less pronounced disability: a person who has lost a leg will be teased less than someone who has a clubfoot. With few exceptions, people with serious disabilities or disfigurements are simply not teased, at least not openly. Most people are aware of the sheer inappropriateness of teasing such people. In addition, people with serious disabilities tend to learn early how to cope with any teasing they may encounter. Whether they laugh it off, devise a comeback that shames the teaser, or don't react at all, the teaser is unlikely to victimize them again.

The people who are most likely to be perpetual victims of teasing or bullying are typically those who respond by crying or showing in some other way how upset they are. These are typically children who are quiet, reserved, and very sensitive to rejection. "The key to the problem is the reaction to being teased or bullied" (Pearce, 1989: 18). Children who are extremely sensitive to taunts and insults set themselves up as targets.

Why Do People Tease?

People tease and bully for a variety of reasons, some more innocent than others. To examine people's motives for teasing, April Watts Brooks and I (1998) asked people to list all the reasons they could think of to explain why people tease. The resulting list was quite diverse: people tease for fun, for attention, to annoy others, to hurt others, to gain dominance, because they are jealous of others, to hide problems or faults, and for many other reasons.

Parents may tease their children to help them develop social skills that will serve them well as they approach the school years and are confronted by peer teasers and bullies. Parents or friends may tease to express intimacy and camaraderie or just to have fun. Parents may also use teasing to control their children's behavior. If their child complains frequently, for example, they may tease him every time he complains as a means of putting an end to the complaining.

One of the most common reasons for teasing or bullying is to promote social conformity. Who can forget the reactions of students in Littleton, Colorado, to the "Trenchcoat Mafia"? People do not react favorably to those who stand out from the crowd. Such individuals are treated as outcasts and ridiculed. Indeed, the number one characteristic believed to motivate bullying is failure to fit in (Hoover and Oliver, 1996).

Furthermore, people may tease those who don't fit in as a way of distancing themselves from something they fear or don't understand. By taunting a stutterer, say, teasers and bullies reassure themselves that the target's problem is not theirs and never will be. Typically a child who stutters is teased through imitation. The teasers, delightedly demonstrating their ability to start and stop stuttering at will, assure themselves and each other that their own speech is perfectly fluent.

Teasing and bullying can be a means of impression management. A girl who wants to be thought of as a friendly kid with a great sense of humor may engage in good-natured teasing. A boy who wants to feel better about himself may divert attention from his personal inadequacies by pointing out other people's flaws. Particularly if he feels socially disadvantaged or is performing poorly at school, he may turn to bullying as a way to engender respect from his peers, even if the respect stems from fear.

Many people tease or bully as a response to teasing or bullying they themselves have suffered (Cohen-Posey, 1995). In these instances, the behavior is a means of seeking revenge. This motive is more common for teasing than for bullying, however, primarily because bullying virtually always occurs between individuals of unequal status: a dominant person bullies a weaker one. The weaker person seldom has an opportunity to turn the tables on the one with more power. When a manager routinely bullies and harasses the subordinate employees, they may look for new jobs, but their responses typically do not include harassing or bullying the boss.

Although it would be unusual for a low-power person to bully a high-power person, bullies often see slights and hostile motives that are simply not there. A bully who is accidentally bumped in the hall by another student is likely to believe that the bump was intentional and to seek revenge.

Victims' vs. Perpetrators' Perceptions of Teasing

The target's perception of teasing, as of other annoying behaviors, often differs from the perpetrator's. Victims view teasing more negatively than perpetrators, perceive it to be motivated by more malice, and view the consequences as more harmful.

Studies on verbal aggressiveness, of which teasing is one type, have found differences in victims' and perpetrators' views of it (Infante et al., 1992). People who are high in verbal aggressiveness perceive teasing and other forms of verbal aggression as less hurtful than people who are low in verbal aggressiveness. This perception may lead them to believe that other people, too, see no harm in their behavior, thus increasing the likelihood that the behavior will continue.

Because I was interested in the magnitude of the difference between victims' and perpetrators' perceptions of teasing, I asked seventy-two students to write two accounts, one describing an incident in which they had been teased (victim stories) and one describing a time when they had teased someone else (perpetrator stories). After writing their accounts, participants answered a series of questions designed to help determine the degree of difference between victims' and perpetrators' views of teasing. Almost half of the victim stories, particularly those written by women, focused on physical appearance. Anita wrote, "When I was younger people picked on me about my nose. They would call me Banana Nose and Pinocchio and ask if they could slide down my nose sometime. Ridiculous stuff, but I was very insecure and it killed me. It was miserable." More than half of the women's stories focused on being teased about their appearance; men were teased equally about their appearance and their relationships (Kowalski, 2000).

When the students wrote about teasing others, appearance came second to behavior as a subject of their confrontations. Male and female perpetrators did not differ in the content of their teases.

These accounts of teasing also showed that victims viewed the experience more negatively than perpetrators and reported more negative effects on their self-esteem. One student wrote,

> Through my last few years of high school my mother teased me about my appearance, describing me as flat-chested, etc. One night at dinner she referred to my "hope chest—which isn't very hopeful." I responded with embarrassment and anger. On the whole, I am satisfied with my appearance, but the size of my chest has always been a touchy subject for me. My mother still teases me about it, though I have made it clear that I don't appreciate her jokes. What she sees as harmless teasing in reality cuts down my self-esteem.

Perpetrators reported more guilt about the experience than victims but also perceived the teasing incident to be more humorous than victims did.

Perpetrators thought their victims liked them better than they actually did, and victims thought the perpetrators disliked them more than they actually did. It is possible that victims misinterpreted the motives of the perpetrators, imputing malice when there was none and believing that the perpetrators valued their relationships less than in fact they did. At the same time, perpetrators may have actually been motivated by ill will toward the victim but either been unwilling to admit it or had forgotten their own motives with the passage of time (Kowalski, 2000).

Consequences of Teasing and Bullying

Depending on how the teasing is perceived and the nature of the relationship between teaser and target, the consequences of teasing can be either positive or negative. On the positive side, teasing can lead to camaraderie and increased intimacy. Good-natured teasing allows people to share a good laugh and to feel a bond with each other. On the negative side, teasing may be perceived as evidence that the teaser thinks little of them and their relationship. People who believe that they are not valued feel rejected and suffer severe loss of self-esteem.

The consequences of bullying, too, can be either favorable or unfavorable. Although bullying rarely has positive consequences for the victim, some victims claim that they are tougher and stronger for having been bullied. Harrison Ford and Tom Cruise have said that they were bullied as children but that they are the better for it now (http://www.bullying.newham.net/stop.htm). In general, the consequences of bullying mirror those of teasing, except that they may be more severe. One reason may be the repetitiveness and sheer abusiveness of most bullying.

VICTIMS OF TEASING AND BULLYING

Good-natured teasing that the victim sees as positive can bring increased feelings of camaraderie with the teaser. Teasing also allows young children to develop social and linguistic skills that will serve them well as they move through adolescence into adulthood. And as virtually everyone can attest, teasing can make for a humorous, enjoyable, lighthearted interaction.

Despite the positive effects that teasing can have, it is the negative consequences that are most memorable and most long-lasting. Short-term negative consequences include feelings of shame, embarrassment, and humiliation. A student who had been teased in junior high school about her bright pink shoes said, "I remember feeling like I wanted to disappear off the face of the earth." Another student who was teased in the first grade said, "I kept it to myself because I was too ashamed. But still today I can remember how bad I felt." One study found that as many as 50 percent of students who had been bullied reported that the bullying had negative effects on their health (Rigby, 1997). Victims may be so anxious about later encounters with the teaser or anyone else who witnessed the teasing that they withdraw from social activities. Finally, victims of teasing may experience such anger that they seek revenge or retaliation against the teaser either immediately or at some time in the future. Patti, a biracial student who was teased in her seventh-grade gym class, reports such feelings: "We had to pick teams for a sport game. Most of the white kids picked white kids and the black kids picked black kids. I was one of the last people standing there. All of a sudden this girl that I would love to meet in a dark alley one day said to me, "So which side are you going to be on?" All of the kids started laughing and her friends were just pointing and laughing at me. I could have killed her."

In response to the rash of school shootings in the 1990s, a high school freshman who called herself an outcast at her school reported: "I would rather be beat up than have those words hurled at me. Bruises heal, but the emotional pain can stay there for years. I mean, if the abuse goes all the way to senior year—people ignoring you, calling you a loser, a fat ass, a freak, whatever—I mean, I could see how that would send someone over the edge and want to blow all their heads off" (Vigue and Rodriguez, 1999).

Other serious consequences of teasing include depression, anxiety, body self-consciousness, loneliness, and low self-esteem. Negative experiences with teasing in early childhood often persist into adulthood. The development of eating disorders in women, for example, is related to a history of being teased about their appearance in childhood (Thompson et al., 1995). My students have consistently reported negative effects of teasing many, many years after the teasing occurred. Suzanne reported,

> I always experienced extreme social anxiety in middle school at lunchtime. The lunchroom was very large, and the entrance required you to walk through or in front of the tables to get your lunch tray in line. I hated it every day and was never sure who I was going to sit with. Obviously, there were social cliques segregating groups and lunch tables. I remember one lunch walking down the middle and feeling extremely embarrassed because the table I usually sat at was full. I heard, "Here comes Gonzo!" and I knew it was directed at me but I didn't get it so I went over to the girl who had called me the name so abrasively loud and sat down (we were sort of friends). I tried to smile and play it off, and I asked why she'd said that, and she said, "You know Gonzo the Muppet with the big nose?" and everyone laughed again. I thought I was going to die. I left my tray and ran to the bathroom. I have always had a complex about my nose being too large. I worry about it all the time. I tried plastic surgery but it didn't work and I can't afford to do it again.

Jerry wrote, "I was waiting for the school bus. I don't remember how old I was, but it was elementary school. A boy who was there asked me why I talked so funny. He said I sounded like I had a lisp. I was devastated. No one ever told me that before, and I continued to be embarrassed for years afterward. I still am self-conscious about speaking sometimes even now."

Finally, Rebecca told of being teased in the third grade:

> The summer before third grade I had braces put on my teeth. The braces made my lips stick out. My lips were already big— thick lips run in my family. In third grade there were a couple of rude boys in my class. One day when my teacher left the classroom, they began picking on me. They started calling me horrible names. On top of that, they started teasing me about my ears. My ears naturally stick out too. I had really long hair in

Table 3.2. Effects of Teasing on Self-Esteem

"Why did you choose to write about this episode of teasing?"

- I chose this episode because it impacted my social life and self-esteem greatly.
- I picked this experience because it was the first incident of being teased about my appearance. I will never forget how low it made me feel about myself.
- It stands out to me like it was yesterday.
- Because physical appearance is very important to me. When someone says something negative about my physical appearance, it greatly hurts my feelings.
- It was the most unforgettable experience of my life.
- It is the aspect that hurts me most and is still causing problems in my life.
- Because I feel that incidents such as these leave permanent scars and are never really forgotten.
- The teasing was a constant occurrence and I still have bad feelings about it.
- It was a horrible experience that I probably will never forget.
- Although I had never considered myself ugly before, after that I became very obsessed with my appearance, and I felt ugly for a long time afterward.

third grade, so my mother pulled it back a lot, making my ears more obvious. So the boys started calling me Dumbo and telling me I'd better watch it or I would fly away. Ever since the third grade, I have been so paranoid about my ears and my lips.

Like most teasing incidents, these episodes happened many, many years earlier, yet they were still having dramatic effects on the lives of the writers. Teasing that could have lasted only a few minutes had affected the lives of the victims ever since. Other comments reflecting the long-term negative consequences of teasing are seen in table 3.2. Students who had written personal narratives about being teased were asked why they had selected the particular incident they did. The comments in table 3.2 reflect these responses.

A consequence that has yet to be considered is damage to the victim's relationship with the perpetrator. Victims who feel that the teasing indicates rejection may distance themselves from the perpetrator to avoid being hurt again. Some victims may be so resentful that they retaliate, as Ben did when he was teased on the school bus in the first grade:

> The older two kids that sat behind me used to tease me. First of all, I was young and easy prey. Second, I sat beside the biggest idiot in our school. So I got teased along with him. The older kids were bullies. They would hit me on the head as hard as they could. I kept it to myself because I was too ashamed. But still today I can remember how bad I felt. I can remember crying on the bus as they hit me over and over, while the bus driver kept driving. But one day I decided not to take it anymore. I got up and beat the hell out of the boy who had teased me. Needless to say, I lost my bus ticket, but I got my revenge.

Many victims go to great lengths to avoid being teased or bullied. Some children avoid school or even change schools in order to escape the ridicule and humiliation. Adults call in sick at work or change jobs in order to escape harassment at the workplace. Some people even downplay any abilities that make them stand out from the crowd for fear of being teased. Georgia had done very well in high school without really trying, but she pretended to find the work difficult. When she was inducted into the National Honor Society, however, she could no longer hide her intelligence. Her classmates teased her and called her Smarty-pants and Bookworm. To prevent the teasing, Georgia said, "I tried even harder to appear dumb, and even ended up leaving the National Honor Society."

If anything positive can come out of people's negative experi-

Teasing and School Shootings

In rare instances, a history of being teased or bullied may lead victims to direct aggression, either toward themselves in the form of suicide or toward their tormentors. An examination of the most publicized school shootings of the late 1990s reveals that many of the shooters reported having been teased and bullied (Leary et al., in press). Luke Woodham, who killed two students and his mother and injured seven other students in Pearl, Mississippi, had been teased about his weight. Michael Carneal, who killed three students in West Paducah, Kentucky, had been called gay in the school newspaper. In Jonesboro, Arkansas, Mitchell Johnson, who, along with Andrew Golden, shot and killed a teacher and four students, reported that he had been teased about his weight. Eric Harris and Dylan Klebold, who killed a teacher and twelve students at Columbine High School in Littleton, Colorado, were treated as outcasts and teased by school athletes. Within a few hours of the Columbine shooting in April 1999, a high school student named Gerardo Lopez, who had been regularly bullied by his classmates, committed suicide. Fearing that he, too, might reach the breaking point and take out his rage on the bullies who rejected him, he decided to take his own life instead. In 1993 an eighth-grader named Curtis Taylor killed himself to escape repeated bullying by his classmates. That same year, fifteen-year-old Brian Head shot himself to death in front of his classmates (Marano, 1998). And the list goes on.

Because of the role that teasing has played in so many school shootings, school and community officials have recommended ways to eliminate teasing and bullying. The state of Georgia even passed an antibully law in response to the shooting of a student on a school bus and the suicide of another who had been repeatedly bullied. The law stipulates that a student who perpetrates three bullying episodes will be sent to an alternative school. Such laws are a step in the right direction, but they do little to help kids who are being bullied regularly but have been threatened with worse if they tell. These bullies are immune to the antibully law unless someone else is brave enough to tell. Furthermore, even in the absence of threats, many victims are too embarrassed by their victimhood to disclose the bullying to someone in a position to intervene.

ences with teasing, it is likely to be the development of empathy with other victims of teasing, so that they are unlikely to become teasers themselves. Anita, who told about being called Banana Nose and Pinocchio, wrote, "I have grown into my nose now and do not feel so insecure about the way I look. I learned from that, though. Remembering how bad it made me feel, I would not want to cause someone else the same feelings of pain and loneliness."

PERPETRATORS OF TEASING AND BULLYING

Like their victims, perpetrators may experience both positive and negative consequences. For them, though, the positive typically outweighs the negative. They may bolster their self-esteem by putting someone else down, or they may revel in sadistic glee at seeing other people embarrassed, humiliated, and upset. In any case, by focusing on other people's faults, bullies draw attention away from any flaws in themselves that might invite ridicule.

Not all of the consequences to perpetrators are positive, of course. Indeed, many teasers and even some bullies report feelings of guilt, embarrassment, or regret, particularly when their good intentions have backfired and the target was hurt or humiliated. Feelings of guilt are reflected in Vivian's account: "When I was in fifth grade, I had a classmate named Judy. She was probably in a lower socioeconomic group than my friends and I. She was rather big for a ten-year-old, so everybody called her Big Fat Judy. What made it even worse was that she didn't use deodorant, so we would make fun of her for smelling bad, too. Now, when I look back, I feel guilty. She moved during or after fifth grade. I haven't seen her since. I hope she's tall, beautiful, and really successful." That a perpetrator should later admit feelings of guilt and embarrassment is somewhat surprising. To keep their own self-esteem intact, one might expect perpetrators to downplay any negative effects that their teasing might have had on others or any negative feelings their own teasing might have generated in themselves.

Hard-core perpetrators may become so habituated to teasing and bullying that they are desensitized to their victims' pain. Taunts and put-downs just become part of the perpetrator's normal behavioral repertoire. Children for whom bullying becomes habitual are more likely than others to become criminals as adults (Kindlon and Thompson, 1999).

Meanwhile, bullies are rejected over time by their peers. To avoid being bullied themselves, their peers may give every appearance of liking them, but ratings of bullies by their peers show that they are very much disliked and become more so as time goes on. By the time a peer group reaches high school age, bullies are social isolates, valued only by other bullies. Even though they may once have viewed themselves as king of the hill and socially skilled, their self-esteem dwindles over time as their peers increasingly shun them.

THE EFFECTS ON OBSERVERS

Bullying or malicious teasing seldom occurs in private; other people are present to observe it in 85 percent of cases (Marano, 1998). Witnesses have three choices: they can intervene on behalf of the victim, they can side with the perpetrator and join in the harassment, or they can do nothing. The choice depends on one's own history of being ridiculed, one's relationship with the victim and with the perpetrator, one's perception of the teasing as good-natured or hurtful, and one's view of its effect on the victim. The response selected also determines the consequences for the witness.

Witnesses who decide to intervene on behalf of the victim may feel good about their decision to support someone in need of help. It is more likely, however, that they will worry about becoming victims themselves. Defending someone who is being ridiculed puts one's own social status in jeopardy.

Witnesses who join in the teasing may have a good time at the victim's expense with little risk of suffering the same fate, at least not just now. But they may feel guilty if the victim is clearly being made to feel miserable.

Witnesses who do nothing may appear to have opted for the safest response. They are unlikely to be victimized themselves in retaliation for siding with the victim, and they avoid any feelings of guilt for siding with the perpetrator. Witnesses who do nothing, however, do not escape feelings of guilt for having done nothing. These are among the memories that make one cringe.

What Can Be Done about Teasing and Bullying?

Solutions to teasing and bullying are not easy to find. One of the biggest problems is that many parents, teachers, and other authority figures view teasing as a normal part of childhood, particularly for boys—a phase they have to go through, like a rite of passage. "Boys will be boys," they say, shaking their heads but smiling as they say it. But if teasing and bullying are such a normal part of growing up, why are our memories of such episodes so vivid and so painful?

Parents may also be reluctant to acknowledge that their child is either a victim or a perpetrator for fear of being found wanting as parents. The failure of teachers, too, to provide support to children who are being teased and bullied puts the victims in double jeopardy. Not only are they victimized by the perpetrators, but they are hurt by the seeming lack of concern shown by people they should be able to look to for support.

Of course, we're assuming here that the child even told his parents or teachers about the teasing or bullying. Many children are reluctant to report their victimization for fear of setting themselves up for further ridicule and humiliation. Nobody likes a tattletale.

The Bullying Prevention Handbook (Hoover and Oliver, 1996) suggests a number of interventions that may work to reduce the incidence of teasing and bullying: role playing, reverse role playing, behavioral contracting, self-monitoring, assertiveness training for the victims, peer mediation sessions at school, and social skills training.

Many parents use role playing to help their children arm themselves with responses designed to throw the bully off stride. For example, parents may role-play clever responses that the child can offer to an individual who is teasing or bullying him. In reverse role playing, victims and perpetrators are asked to switch roles in an effort to help victims understand the perpetrators' motives and to help teasers and bullies develop empathy for their victims. Behavioral contracts are negotiated with bullies. Specific guidelines are provided, and the bully agrees to cease any kind of bullying. Each violation of the contract will bring a specified punishment. Self-monitoring is a way for teasers and bullies to become sensitized to the magnitude of their behavioral problem. In view of the frequency with which some people tease others, many people could benefit from a short period of self-monitoring or observation of their behavior. Not only would they come to recognize how often they tease others, but they would become sensitized to the reactions of their victims. For the victims, assertiveness training and social skills training are often useful. When we remember that many victims are teased because they are socially inept (they don't fit in), the benefits of social skills training become obvious. Assertiveness training is designed to help victims learn to stand up to their tormentors and to respond in ways that do not invite further victimization. Finally, peer mediation sessions are opportunities for victims and perpetrators to come together and air their feelings and grievances in a controlled, safe environment.

The help offered by such programs reaches beyond the victims and perpetrators they target. Other children are more likely to risk intervening on behalf of the underdog when the school or community has enhanced awareness of the problem by providing a workshop or bully prevention program. Such programs make parents, teachers, and community members, too, aware of the prevalence of teasing and bullying, the seriousness of the problem, and strategies for intervening to help both victim and bully.

Further community support for victims of teasing and bullying can be supplied by a crisis hotline that allows children unlimited access to trained professional counselors. A hotline in England called Childline received so many calls from children who were being bullied that a separate line called the Bullying Line was established (Ross, 1996). Between its founding in 1986 and 2001, Childline had received over a million calls related to bullying (<http://www.childline.org.uk/wekcome/kids.htm>). Some schools have bully boxes where students can leave notices about bullying they have experienced or witnessed. Eye-opening news about bullying and links to resources in many countries, including the United States, can be found at <http://www.success unlimited.co.uk/bullycide/chldnews.htm>.

4

•••••••

Egocentrism, Arrogance, and Conceit

Self-esteem is all very well, but Donna thinks it can be carried too far:

> During the last month of my senior year in high school, I got set up with a junior named Jake. Everyone said that he was so cute and so sweet. Well, at first he was, but as I got to know him, I found out that he had a very big ego. He was constantly looking at himself in the mirror and asking me how he looked. He kept reminding me how lucky I was that he had chosen me as his girlfriend out of his long list of prospects. Our relationship did not last long. When I broke up with him, he was shocked. His attitude was "How could you find someone better than me?" and "Oh, well, I'll snap my fingers and get the next girl on my list."

Most people would be put off at once by the way Jake behaved. His arrogance is unquestionably annoying. Indeed, one researcher has referred to snobbishness and egotism as "two of the most obnoxious of all the personality traits" (Carroll, 1931: 167). Yet isn't a favorable opinion of oneself a good thing? Haven't psychologists touted the importance of high self-esteem? Aren't people who think well of themselves more likely to succeed than people who think little of themselves? In fact, self-esteem and how to nurture it are among the most frequently researched and talked-about topics in psychology. A quick look at the self-help section of any bookstore or a search of the Internet will confirm most people's belief that high self-esteem is essential to a happy life. Amazon.com lists close to three thousand titles that deal with self-esteem, every one of them extolling its virtues. Among them are *The Winning Family: Increasing Self-Esteem in Your Children and Yourself; 501 Ways to Boost Your Child's Self-Esteem; 101 Ways to Make Your Child Feel Special; How to Give Your Child a Great Self-Image.* One book rashly touts itself as "the only book that fully deals with the one most important element to building true happiness and success: positive self-esteem." Parents and teachers alike are encouraged to do everything they can to boost their children's self-esteem, on the assumption that high self-esteem will cure most of what ails children today.

Certainly no one would deny that high self-esteem does have its advantages. People with high self-esteem have the confidence to persist in the face of difficulties that might make others stop trying. If their efforts yield disappointing results, they seem not to sink into despair, in large part because they take credit for their successes but deny responsibility for failure. They also recall positive information about themselves more easily than negative information, and they believe that positive adjectives describe them better than negative adjectives (Brown, 1991; Taylor and Brown, 1988). All in all, people with high self-esteem seem to have somewhat better mental health than those whose self-esteem is low.

Interestingly, most people feel pretty good about themselves. In fact, most people see themselves as better than the average person and have a more positive view of themselves than other people do (Brown, 1991; Taylor and Brown, 1988). These tendencies are referred to as positive illusions, or the Lake Wobegon effect, after Garrison Keillor's fictional town in which "all the children are above average."

Although maintaining a positive self-image may be beneficial to our mental health, it can be carried too far, as anyone who has had anything to do with an arrogant, egotistical snob can attest. Participants in one of my studies put arrogance on a par with betrayal: arrogance not only hurts its targets but brings its own punishment, as we shall see.

Egocentrism, Egotism, and Narcissism

The arrogant are called many things, none of them complimentary: egocentric, cocky, egotistical, snobbish, and narcissistic are among the kinder things we call them. All these terms are applied to people who think they are better than the rest of us. They claim they are smarter or more talented than they really are or more talented than someone else (Leary et al., 1997). Thus, unlike people who simply have high self-esteem and feel good about themselves, people who are egotistical or snobbish believe in their inherent superiority to other people. One of my students described her interactions with another student who was enrolled in the honors college. Every time they saw each other, the other student mentioned something about the honors college. According to my student, "We couldn't even hold a conversation . . . like she was so much better than me."

"Narcissism" is so frequently used to refer to arrogance that I will use the terms interchangeably. According to the *Diagnostic and Statistical Manual of Mental Disorders* (DSM-IV) (American Psychiatric Association, 1994), narcissism combines egotism and selfishness. Narcissists not only claim to be better than they are and better than other people but feel entitled to things they do not deserve. At the same time that they overestimate their own abilities and accomplishments, they underestimate the contributions of others. They view themselves as superior and constantly expect and seek the admiration of others. When narcissists are deprived of the attention and admiration they feel they deserve, they may become angry and demanding.

Developmental Variations in Arrogance and Narcissism

We can all think of people, both young and old, whom we consider arrogant. There do appear to be some developmental variations, however, in the degree of arrogance that people display. Very young children are perhaps the most egocentric of us all, because they are unable to take another person's perspective into account. One of the leading theorists of child psychology, Jean Piaget (1959), suggested that children's egocentrism is not selfishness but rather an inability to view the world from any perspective other than their own.

Although children learn by about the age of eight that their view of the world is not the only view, adolescents seem to have their own type of egocentricity: teenagers have a hard time understanding that an opinion that in any way differs from their own can be valid. They are well aware that other people have other views—wrong ones. Their view of the world is the only right one, and they can be quite intolerant of others' beliefs and perspectives.

Adolescents are also highly egocentric in another way: they tend to believe that they are the center of everyone's attention. When they are out in public, they feel as though all eyes are on them. At this age people are highly self-conscious and concerned about how they appear in others' eyes. They savor approval and admiration at a time when their lives seem to be in turmoil. Adolescents' egocentrism can become exasperating when they believe they are unique in the way they feel and in what they experience. They are quite sure that no one else has ever gone through what they are going through or felt as they do, so no one else could possibly understand. An adolescent in love, for example, is convinced that no one else has ever loved so deeply and so desperately. Trying to convince them of the irrationality of this belief is a constant challenge to parents and teachers (Krantz, 1994).

After adolescence egocentrism appears to decline until it is all but absent among the elderly (Dr. William Chovan, personal communication). The elderly hold views of themselves that are pretty well fixed by this stage of their lives, so they feel less need for other people's approval.

Several theories have been proposed to explain why narcissism develops. In keeping with the psychoanalytic tradition most commonly associated with Sigmund Freud, Otto Kernberg (1975/1985) suggested that narcissism develops in children whose parents have rejected or abandoned them. The children come to believe that they have only themselves to rely on and that other people are not to be trusted. Theodore Millon (1981), on the other hand, argued that narcissism develops not because parents have rejected their children but rather because they have showered them with excessive attention and adulation. Children who become narcissistic are those who have been so overindulged and overpraised that they come to believe that everything they do is perfect. It is the parents who teach these children to have an inflated view of themselves. In investigating why the school performance of American children has declined steadily over recent years, whereas the performance of some immigrant students in the United States and of students in other countries has not, one researcher, Yong Hwang (1995), suggested that American schools have done students a disservice by demonstrating positive regard for them regardless of the level of their accomplishments, giving them higher grades than they merit and promoting them whether they perform well or not. Asian-American students, who reliably outperform students of other national and ethnic backgrounds, are not accustomed to receiving liberal compliments at home. If their parents compliment them, it's because their accomplishments are praiseworthy. "False self-esteem," Hwang says, "leads to narcissistic self-intoxication" (487).

Regardless of which theory is correct, age typically tempers people's narcissistic tendencies, at least to a point. Children who have been devalued by their parents eventually forge relationships with other people whom they can learn to trust. Over time, children who have been overpraised by their parents are knocked off their pedestals by other people, so that eventually they come to have a more realistic view of themselves.

How Do We Detect Egotism?

Almost everyone appears to have a touch of narcissism or arrogance at times. Indeed, "normal" narcissism has been described as "an essential constituent for most human functioning because it involves the self-preserving, self-regulating, and self-asserting activities" (Stone, 1998: 7). Because most people have at least passing familiarity with narcissism, it typically is not difficult to spot arrogance when someone claims abilities of which we have seen no evidence or who repeatedly ignores or rejects criticisms (Schutz, 1998). Two researchers (Hallmark and Curtis, 1994) concluded that "arrogance is not an attitude, peculiarity, or personal trait, but an external public evaluation of a public performance." In other words, people judge our claims regarding our abilities by the abilities we have demonstrated.

When we have little information to go by, judging that someone is arrogant or narcissistic may be more difficult, but people do it all the time. If you ask them how they know, they typically say that such people just have an air about them. But what is it that creates this air or aura of egotism?

Since most people know enough not to go about extolling their virtues, when we call someone arrogant, we must be basing our judgment on other cues. But what cues? No research has directly examined this question. It has been suggested that inferences regarding egotism may be based in part on the role an individual plays. People who put themselves in the public eye and are well paid in money and adulation—rock stars and sports stars, say—are almost universally thought to be arrogant. When a superstar turns out to be likable and humble after all, we are pleasantly surprised.

What other cues might lead us to infer that someone is arrogant? Most people assume that arrogant individuals carry themselves in a particular way. They walk with great confidence, with their heads held high and with their chests thrust slightly forward. They move purposefully and without hesitation (Leary et al., 1997). They often show disdain for or disinterest in others. Consider the experience of a neighbor of mine. She has a college classmate who lives very well indeed, in a large home with a staff of servants to attend to her every need. When my neighbor dropped in for a friendly chat with her old friend one day, the butler announced through the intercom that madam was not receiving visitors that day. Almost anyone in that situation would perceive the woman as arrogant in the extreme.

Some people assume that an upper-class British accent conveys arrogance—and so it may, if the person who uses it is neither upper class nor British. A Vermont boy who wins a Rhodes scholarship for study at Oxford and is still speaking with an Oxford accent back home at forty is not likely to endear himself to his associates. My student Kathy wrote, "When I was a freshman in college, I dated the most arrogant guy ever. He always made it clear that he was better than everyone else. One specific habit he had was talking in a British accent. No one enjoyed listening to him speak with that accent because it made them feel inferior to him. Oddly, however, no one ever confronted him about how it annoyed them. He still continues to use this accent, and he is still annoyingly arrogant."

Even without assuming an accent, people may pronounce certain words in ways that lead others to perceive them as arrogant. People, particularly in the United States, who say "tomahto" instead of "tomayto" or "vahz" instead of "vayz" tend to be viewed as haughty and in need of being brought down a notch or two.

Regardless of the specific cues people use to determine that someone is arrogant, we all seem to just know. It would seem, then, that if we can detect egotism and arrogance in others, we should be able to detect arrogance in ourselves if we could view ourselves as others do. Just such behavior was observed among some of the fifteen people who, one by one, were voted off the *Survivor* TV show during its first season by the others who were "stranded" together on a remote island. Although certainly physical stamina played a role in the contestants' ability to endure from week to week, some reports suggested that the greatest endurance was needed to survive the egos of the other castaways. The morning after the contestants were voted off, they were interviewed on CBS's *Early Show*. As they watched video clips of their interactions with others on the island, many expressed chagrin at seeing how annoying they were. Once they were in a position to observe their own behavior, they could perceive arrogance in themselves as readily as in other people. The only person who did not make such comments was the winner, Richard Hatch. When he heard that other castaways described him as controlling, conniving, devious, manipulative, and mean, Hatch responded that he preferred to describe himself as influential rather than manipulative. He had simply done what he had to do on the island, he told reporters; he was really not concerned about what the others thought of him.

Why Egotism Is Annoying

If, as research on positive illusions suggests, most people perceive themselves to be better than average, why do we see egotism as so annoying? Mark Leary and his colleagues (1997) have pointed to six reasons: it threatens our self-esteem, it is seen as misrepresentation, it is exploitative and manipulative, it is associated with defensiveness, it is seen as illegitimate, and it leads to boredom.

THREATS TO OTHER PEOPLE'S SELF-ESTEEM

People who claim to be better than others are implying that other people are inferior to them. Another person's egotism, then, comes across to us as an insult: our own ideas, opinions, and abilities are being called into question. Because self-esteem is so highly valued, any threat to our self-esteem will be obnoxious to us. If another person's egotistical claims lead you to question your own abilities, your self-esteem will be lowered, as Ted discovered: "In middle school I had to wear a back brace. I had really low self-esteem. I honestly felt like everybody was arrogant and conceited compared to me. Even some of my best friends from elementary school were acting different toward me. They would laugh when they thought I couldn't hear and say things to me to emphasize how "cool" or "popular" they were. I will never forget the way they acted. It had a big effect on my life."

That egotists themselves are aware of their effects on another person's self-esteem is reflected in Amy's story: "I think I acted arrogantly toward a girl when we were trying out for cheerleading my junior year of high school. All week during tryouts I think I made myself seem better than her. I never meant to do that. I am sure it made her feel really terrible. I felt even worse when I made it and she didn't. I really haven't talked to her much since then. I can't imagine her wanting to talk to me after the way I made her feel."

MISREPRESENTATION

The participants in any interaction expect the other participants to be who and what they say they are. And indeed, most people try to behave in ways that are consistent with what others already know about them (Baumeister and Jones, 1978). People whose claims are inconsistent with their true selves or who exaggerate their abilities are perceived to be misrepresenting themselves and are evaluated negatively. When we must interact with egotistical people, we have to decide how to behave. Should we respond to them as we know them to be or as they portray themselves?

ENTITLEMENT AND EXPLOITATION

A sense of entitlement and manipulation are defining character-istics of the narcissist. Because narcissistic persons view them-selves as superior to others, they believe they are owed special treatment. They see their own ideas as so superior that they often use unconventional or unethical means to manipulate and per-suade others that their way is the right way (Carroll, 1931).

Narcissism is not limited to individuals; we find it in groups and nations as well. Mark Leary and his colleagues (1997) note that "some of the worst cases of exploitation in history can be traced to one group's belief that it was superior to another, and, thus, had a right to treat the supposedly inferior group as it de-sired. The subjugation of slaves, the domination of Native Amer-icans, apartheid in South Africa, and the Holocaust all involved the egotistical belief that, due to their superiority, some people had a right to exploit others" (121).

DEFENSIVENESS

Because criticism challenges narcissists' view of themselves, they do not respond well to it. Indeed, denying that any criticism di-rected at them can have any merit is one thing that leads us to infer that they are arrogant in the first place. In their minds, the judgment of anyone so inferior as not to recognize their superi-ority is not worth considering.

ILLEGITIMATE SELF-ESTEEM

People who have worked hard and done well have a right to feel good about themselves. Few of us begrudge the triumphant joy of Olympic athletes displaying their gold medals. The Olympians we tend to disdain are the sore losers, the ones who belittle the winners or angrily refuse the silver medal or in any other way indicate that they think the gold medal should have been theirs. Athletes who claim it's the coach's fault that they didn't make the team are scorned. They are attempting to bolster their self-esteem by claiming ability they do not have.

BOREDOM

Most of us are more interested in ourselves than in other people. Thus we become bored when other people talk about nothing but themselves. Typically there is no give and take in such conversations. Our role is to listen or to provide an echo. As the old joke goes, "But enough about me. Tell me, what do *you* think about me?"

Why Behave Egotistically?

Why, when egotism is so universally disliked, do people choose to behave egotistically? One reason may be that egotists truly believe that they are as good as they say they are. They are stunned when others don't view them as favorably as they view themselves (Leary et al., 1997). Typically, egotists who believe that their claims are legitimate have received excessive praise and adoration, either as children or as adults. Parents who praise all of their child's undertakings without differentiating between effort and accomplishment are conveying the message that everything the child does is exceptional.

In the course of growing up, however, even such a child should have absorbed enough basic social skills to recognize that it doesn't do to go around blowing your own horn. That's elementary to most people, yet egotists' claims are rarely challenged. Seldom would someone say to a self-aggrandizer, "That's not true. You aren't nearly as good as you think you are." Although holding your tongue serves to keep the peace, it does nothing to curb the egotist's claims.

Not every egotist, though, believes those claims. Many people deliberately exaggerate their abilities in efforts to control other people's perceptions of them. People who are perceived as competent are better liked and are assigned more responsibilities than those who are perceived as incompetent. Thus, to the extent that exaggerated claims help us to be perceived as competent but not as braggarts, we may convey the impression that we are better than we really are. There are two problems with this strategy, however. First, if you exaggerate your abilities, you run the risk of being found out eventually. At that point, you may still be perceived as competent but you will surely be seen as a liar. In any case, making exaggerated claims without appearing conceited requires a degree of social skill that very few people possess. Second, although we value competence, extraordinary competence can make us feel uneasy. This is where a phenomenon known as the pratfall effect comes in (Taylor, Peplau, and Sears, 2000). An egotist who makes a highly public blunder suffers humiliation; but if a highly competent person makes a blunder—if the secretary of state spills his wine at a dinner for a visiting dignitary, say— we tend actually to like him more. Why, we think, he's not so different from us after all!

People may behave arrogantly because doing so has redeeming value in some circumstances. Despite the inclusion of narcissistic personality disorder in the DSM-IV (American Psychiatric Association, 1994), researchers have suggested that some aspects of narcissism—leadership/authority, superiority/arrogance, and self-absorption/self-admiration—may sometimes be adaptive (Hill and Yousey, 1998). Only exploitativeness/entitlement appears to be consistently maladaptive. People with favorable views of themselves persist at tasks longer and take on more challenging tasks than those who think less highly of themselves.

Some features of narcissism prepare people for occupations that subject them to a significant amount of social attention, such as political office (Hill and Yousey, 1998). Ronald Deluga (1997) found narcissism to be related to charismatic leadership among American presidents. He found that Franklin Roosevelt was rated as the most charismatic president and ranked second in narcissism. Roosevelt was extremely self-confident and conveyed a clear air of superiority. At times he was manipulative, but he was an effective leader at a time when the nation needed a strong hand at the helm—-during the Great Depression and World War II. People who do well in sales positions rate high in narcissism (Soyer et al., 1999). Presumably the outgoing and gregarious personality of a narcissist serves a salesperson very well. The adaptiveness of a narcissistic characteristic in an occupational setting, however, does not in any way imply that it is also adaptive in interpersonal relationships. Indeed, pathological narcissism has been identified as a characteristic of serial killers (Schlesinger, 1998). And the narcissism that enhances charismatic leadership is not always adaptive, as Jim Jones, the charismatic leader of the People's Temple, amply demonstrated in 1978. Having persuaded his followers to move from California to Guyana, he then commanded, cajoled, and coerced them to take their own lives by drinking Kool-Ade laced with cyanide. The death toll was 913.

Sigmund Freud (1914/1957) described narcissism as a way to ward off feelings of depression and low self-esteem. Thus narcissism may be self-protective. One of the great ironies of this annoying behavior is that narcissists tend to succeed at most of their undertakings. Part of their success may stem from their extreme fear of failing or losing the admiration of their associates. And although you might expect their interpersonal relationships to be compromised (sometimes they are, of course), many people seem to be drawn to narcissists. Perhaps people who are not themselves narcissists admire narcissists' ability to promote themselves (Freud, 1914/1957). Nonnarcissists may use their connections with narcissists to enhance their own self-esteem. We tend to revel in our affiliations with successful people, basking in reflected glory.

Consequences of Excessive Narcissism

Both high self-esteem and narcissism can have beneficial consequences, but the two should not be confused. People with high self-esteem have favorable views of themselves that are relatively

---

Are You a Narcissist?

Since all of us have at some time claimed to be better than we are, researchers have developed self-report measures to determine how narcissistic we really are. One of the most frequently used self-report measures is the Narcissistic Personality Inventory (NPI) (Emmons, 1987; Raskin and Hall, 1979) (see table 4.1). The original NPI, consisting of fifty-four items to which participants responded in a forced-choice format, was revised in 1987 to yield a measure with thirty-seven items to which participants respond in a true-false format. You can get a feel for your own level of narcissism by responding true or false to each of the items on the NPI. For each "true" response, give yourself a score of 1. For each "false" response, assign a value of 0. Then simply sum your scores. The higher your score, the greater your tendency toward narcissism.

stable in the face of insults or other threats to the self. Egotists' favorable views of themselves are not so resilient. Indeed, their self-esteem is considered to be high but fragile (Kernis et al., 1989). They are very sensitive to anything that may in any way threaten their self-satisfaction. Unlike egotists, people with high self-esteem typically display humility, which Robert Emmons (2000) defines as the ability "to see oneself as basically equal with any other human being even if there are objective differences in physical beauty, wealth, social skills, intelligence, or other resources" (164). Given the instability of egotists' high self-esteem, most of the consequences of egotism are negative, both for the egotists themselves and for people with whom they interact.

One of the most immediate interpersonal consequences of egotism is hurt feelings. Arrogance makes us feel belittled. When other people assume that they are better or more deserving than we, the implication is that they consider us to have little value. People who put us down cannot put a very high value on their relationship with us. These feelings of hurt were reflected in many of my students' narratives:

> I used to dance in a competitive dance company. A girl in the company was very egotistic. She was a good dancer, but she knew it. One night we were going over a routine, and I kept messing up on one particular part. She tried to correct me but I still didn't understand. She got frustrated and said, "I don't know why they let people like you in this company. Only people as good as me should be allowed.' When she put me down that way, I felt crushed."

> Last semester I had a class with a girl who was a genius at making me feel bad. When we were put into the same group for a group project, she would just dismiss any idea of mine as if I had never mentioned it. She always made me feel so stupid, not only in class but outside it too. Occasionally I would see her on campus and I would smile and say hi, but she never answered. She completely ignored me. She made me feel like nothing.

Table 4.1. Narcissistic Personality Inventory

Respond to each of the following items with a T (for true) or an F (for false).

_____   1. I see myself as a good leader.
_____   2. I like to look at my body.
_____   3. I usually dominate any conversation.
_____   4. I expect a great deal from other people.
_____   5. I would prefer to be a leader.
_____   6. I like to look at myself in the mirror.
_____   7. I can make anybody believe anything.
_____   8. I am envious of other people's good fortune.
_____   9. I really like to be the center of attention.
_____   10. I am an extraordinary person.
_____   11. I am a born leader.
_____   12. I insist upon getting the respect that is due me.
_____   13. I like having authority over other people.
_____   14. I like to display my body.
_____   15. I can read people like a book.
_____   16. I will never be satisfied until I get all that I deserve.
_____   17. I would be willing to describe myself as a strong personality.
_____   18. I have good taste when it comes to beauty.
_____   19. I am apt to show off if I get the chance.

When other people's egotism arouses negative feelings in us, we not only avoid them but lose respect for them: "After I walked in on my fiancé with another woman, he seemed to think he had proved he was irresistible. When I refused to continue to see him, he became so arrogant that no one could be around him. All he could talk about was what kind of 'man' he was, what a 'heartbreaker' he was. What he didn't realize was that every time he talked about what he did, people looked at him with no respect."

Egotism has a way of leading to conflict. People who have an inflated sense of themselves are frequently frustrated when others fail to recognize their superiority. Because their views of themselves are at odds with other people's views of them, the stage is

_____ 20. I have a strong will to power.

_____ 21. I have a natural talent for influencing people.

_____ 22. I think I am a special person.

_____ 23. People can learn a great deal from me.

_____ 24. I get upset when people don't notice how I look when I go out in public.

_____ 25. I like to be the center of attention.

_____ 26. I like to be complimented.

_____ 27. I always know what I am doing.

_____ 28. I find it easy to manipulate people.

_____ 29. I am assertive.

_____ 30. I am going to be a great person.

_____ 31. I can usually talk my way out of anything.

_____ 32. I am more capable than other people.

_____ 33. People always seem to recognize my authority.

_____ 34. I know that I am good because everyone keeps telling me so.

_____ 35. Superiority is something you are born with.

_____ 36. Everybody likes to hear my stories.

_____ 37. I would do almost anything on a dare.

Source: R. A. Emmons, "Narcissism: Theory and Measurement," *Journal of Personality and Social Psychology* 52 (1987): 11–17. Copyright © by the American Psychological Association. Adapted with permission.

set for conflict. As Carl Malmquist (1996) has written, "Slights, such as a tone of criticism by another person or not being placed in a position of special importance in some interpersonal relationship or at work, can become sources of brooding. Rage, shame, guilt, and humiliation emerge subsequent to these perceived slights, although they may be hidden under an attempted exterior of indifference" (164–65).

Conflict may also result when egocentrism leads people to take more credit than they deserve (Gilovich, Medvec, and Savitsky, 1998; Gilovich et al., 1999). Imagine that you and your significant other have divided responsibility for household chores, and the two of you are asked to estimate the percentage of chores you do.

If you are like other people who have completed this exercise (Ross and Sicoly, 1979), you will find that you or your partner or both claim responsibility for a disproportionate share of the work. If you and your partner did all the work each of you claims, the proportions would add up to over 100 percent, a practical impossibility.

One reason people do this is that they are more aware of their own contributions to joint activities than they are of the contributions of their partner (Gilovich, Medvec, and Savitsky, 1998). Although you are aware of each time you scoop out the cat's litter box, you are not necessarily aware of the times your partner does it, so you overestimate your share of the responsibility and underestimate your partner's share.

People who feel that they are doing more than their share in a relationship are likely to feel angry and resentful. Confrontations will be fruitless because both partners believe they are doing more than their fair share and that the other partner has no right to demand more of them. Each partner may perceive malicious intent in the other when in fact none was intended. In other words, each partner may assume incorrectly that the other is not making an honest error in judgment but rather is trying to gain some personal advantage.

Conflict may also follow from egotists' illusion of transparency (Gilovich, Savitsky, and Medvec, 1998)—their belief that their thoughts and feelings are more apparent to others than they actually are. When people believe they have communicated their feelings clearly when in fact they have not, the scene is set for conflict. If you believe you have made it clear to your significant other that his failure to phone you when he's going to be late fills you with righteous indignation, yet he goes right on showing up late without phoning, it will seem to you that your feelings don't matter to him at all, and your relationship may be jeopardized. It is possible, though, that you haven't communicated your feelings as clearly as you thought.

The illusion of transparency can have negative consequences for the egotist, too, when a self-exacerbating syndrome develops (Storms and McCaul, 1976). A self-exacerbating syndrome consists of negative thoughts and feelings that are made worse by fear that others are aware of them. Many people become anxious when they have to speak in public, for example, but if you think other people can see how nervous you are, you'll be more nervous still.

Other negative personal consequences of egotism follow from the spotlight effect—the assumption that one's actions are more conspicuous to others than they actually are (Gilovich, Medvec, and Savitsky, 1998). Because we are generally so highly aware of what we are doing, we may assume that others are paying just as much attention to it as we are. A person dining alone in a restaurant, for instance, may feel self-conscious, convinced that all the other diners are thinking, "There's somebody who has no friends." That's why many people take a book or a legal pad when they must dine alone and try to appear busily engaged in studying or writing—too preoccupied by important business to socialize.

In a very interesting study to demonstrate the spotlight effect (Gilovich, Medvec, and Savitsky, 1998), participants were asked to wear an oversized T-shirt adorned with a picture of Barry Manilow. The participants were then instructed to proceed down the hall and to knock on a designated door. Upon doing so, the participant was greeted by another experimenter and five other participants. The experimenter asked the participant to wait outside for a few minutes. Shortly the experimenter joined the participant in the hallway and asked several questions, one of which was how many of the five people in the room the participant thought could identify the face on the T-shirt. On average, participants estimated that approximately 50 percent of the five had noticed the picture of Barry Manilow when in fact only 25 percent had done so. We don't really have to be narcissists to believe that other people are more keenly aware of us than they generally are.

Narcissism and Aggression

The traditional view of aggression was that it was associated with low self-esteem. Recently, however, Roy Baumeister and his colleagues (Baumeister, 1997; Baumeister, Bushman, and Campbell, 2000; Baumeister and Campbell, 1999) have argued that because egotists' self-esteem is unstable, they are more likely to be aggressive in the face of some threat to the ego. First, egotists are extremely sensitive to criticism, personal affront, or insult. Believing themselves to be superior to others, they find it hard to imagine how anyone could fail to admire them. Think of the alternative: if they accepted someone else's unflattering evaluation, they would have to change their perceptions of themselves. A quick review of the characteristics of a narcissist reveals why this alternative is unacceptable. A defining characteristic of narcissism is the need to maintain a favorable view of the self. "People with high self-esteem that is also highly narcissistic have the most to lose from threats to their self-view because their self-view is so wildly favorable. Such threats should also occur with much more frequency because the probability of external disagreement may increase as the self-view becomes more inflated and more unrealistic" (Papps and O'Carroll, 1998: 433).

Second, egotists have difficulty adopting the perspectives of other people, so they have trouble understanding why anyone would want to criticize or insult them.

Third, because they lack empathy and humility and have grandiose fantasies of power, they are likely to respond aggressively to a personal affront. According to Malmquist (1996), "Narcissistic components are present more frequently in homicides than is usually believed. . . . The key seems to be an experience of some type of threat to one's vulnerable self that becomes magnified far beyond the nature of the threat" (174). Theodore Kaczynski, commonly known as the Unabomber, is a prime example. Although it would be difficult to identify the precise threats to Kaczynski's ego or self, many of them probably extending back to his childhood, we do know that his egotistical view of himself as one of the world's greatest mathematicians was challenged. During his tenure as a professor at the University of California at Berkeley, for example, Kaczynski's students regularly criticized him as an ineffective instructor. Similarly, there is some evidence that many of the perpetrators of the school shootings that occurred in the 1990s were narcissists who had been ridiculed by their classmates (Leary et al., in press). The damage to their sense of self-esteem played a large part in propelling these kids toward killing rampages.

Additional data on bullying also supports a connection between egotism and aggression. Despite the initial belief that bullies had low self-esteem and were putting others down as a means of making themselves feel better, research now suggests that the self-esteem of bullies is no lower than that of the average child and may actually be higher (Olweus, 1993). The problem for bullies is that their self-esteem is fragile, so that they are extremely sensitive to criticism and insults.

Excessive egotism may lead people, particularly those in the helping professions—firefighters, police officers, nurses—to set fires, plant bombs, or put patients in distress so that they can be the first to respond and play the hero. As the criminologist Michael Rustigen (1996) has pointed out, such individuals "have a very strong need for attention, and they have monstrous egos. Now, they're going to show the world their importance."

Broadening the Scope of Narcissism

Narcissism may sound like an idiosyncrasy, a personal trait, but its scope is much broader than that. Emmons (1987) discusses narcissism as a "cultural or societal entity." It is not only individuals that are becoming more narcissistic; entire cultures are becoming so, a phenomenon I refer to as "ethnonarcissism." After all, wasn't the counterculture of the 1960s followed by the "me" generation? Isn't the horror of "ethnic cleansing" based on the idea that one ethnic group is better than another? Civil wars break out and international conflicts develop because one country or one group feels superior to another; terrorism is loosed upon the world because one group feels superior to every other. The consequences of narcissism to countries and groups within countries mirror those that befall narcissistic individuals.

How to Tame the Wild Ego

People who are egotists or narcissists are likely to remain so, at least to some degree, for the rest of their lives. Because they view themselves as superior to others, they do not accept any negative feedback telling them that they need to change their ways. Even failure to get a promotion or to win or keep the person they love—any event that presumably would cause the rest of us to stop and think—seems to have little effect. Egotists simply attribute their disappointments to someone else—anyone but themselves.

This is not to imply that the narcissist's situation is completely hopeless. In essence, narcissism is a failure in self-regulation. Narcissists have difficulty withholding statements or behaviors that make themselves appear superior to everyone else. Such statements and behaviors make up the essence of their sense of self. Like people afflicted with other failures in self-regulation, however, narcissists can learn to hold their behavior in check. Just as parents who attempt to turn their children into geniuses to enhance their own self-image—the phenomenon has been referred to as "instrumental narcissism" (Elkind, 1991)—can learn to allow their children to develop at their own pace, so individuals who manifest narcissism can learn to control their behavior.

Narcissists can learn to adopt a more realistic view of their strengths and weaknesses. They can learn to distinguish abilities at which they truly do excel from those that they find more difficult. They can then learn to adopt a more realistic view of themselves so that they will be less sensitive to threats or insults. Even without help in learning to regulate their behavior, many narcissists have their snobbishness knocked out of them by the responses it provokes. In a majority of situations, most people are simply unwilling to tolerate arrogant behavior for very long. After enough rejections, narcissists may eventually decide that the game isn't worth the cost and stop annoying people—at least in that particular way.

5

• • • • • • • •

Incivility and Breaches
of Propriety

It's ten in the morning and you are hard at work on a project that is due at four in the afternoon. In addition to constant interruptions by phone and e-mail messages, one of your colleagues continually interrupts your progress to chat.

Your significant other, despite your repeated admonitions, continually tells embarrassing stories about you in public.

The person in the car ahead of you is driving 20 miles an hour below the posted speed limit, and even at that speed is weaving slightly over the yellow line, so that it is virtually impossible for you to pass. As you edge closer, you see that the driver is talking on a cell phone.

You've called a friend with whom you have not talked in some time. Although you are paying for a long-distance call, your friend puts you on hold three times to accept another call.

A mother and little boy are in front of you in the checkout line at the supermarket. When the mother tells the child to put back the candy he has snatched from the display, the child launches into a tirade studded with profanity and suggestions of improbable places for his mother to put the candy.

Collectively such behaviors are demonstrations of improprieties, incivility, lack of etiquette, rudeness, breaches of propriety, and disrespect. Although we are all familiar with breaches of propriety (our own and other people's) and have become increasingly so over the past decade or two (Buchinger, 1999; Grossman, 1999; Miller, 2001), until recently little attention was devoted to the topic. Many questions remain unanswered: What is incivility, and why do people behave in these ways? Have people always behaved so rudely? What are the most common breaches of propriety? What causes people to be rude? What are the consequences of incivility? What can we do to become more civil?

Defining Incivility

Like most other annoying behaviors, incivility is difficult to define. One person's rudeness is another person's humor. An additional problem is that there are really two types of civility: strict adherence to cultural norms, commonly referred to as etiquette, and acts of kindness and consideration. American etiquette prescribes the use of "sir" and "ma'am" as terms of courtesy and respect, the writing of thank-you notes for gifts received, and the offer of a gentleman's arm to a lady he is escorting. Civility as etiquette is easily taught, in cotillion classes if necessary, and becomes habitual. Civility as an act of kindness requires much more conscious effort, for one must put one's own desires and needs temporarily on hold.

Certainly, these two types of civility often overlap. Waiting for a funeral procession to pass before proceeding on your way, although a rule of etiquette, could also be interpreted as an act of kindness. Usually, however, the two types of civility are distinct, although current definitions tend to combine them: civility has been defined as "the sum of the many sacrifices we are called to make for the sake of living together" (Carter, 1998: 11); incivility has been defined as "acting rudely or discourteously without re-

gard for others, in violation of norms of respect in social interaction" (Andersson and Pearson, 1999: 455).

Regardless of how civility is defined, the intention behind incivility is often ambiguous (Andersson and Pearson, 1999). Fig-
uring out whether another person was intentionally rude or didn't
mean to be insensitive can be difficult. The target of an impropriety may interpret it as intentional rudeness when in fact it was
accidental. For the perpetrator the ambiguity can be an advantage.
Perpetrators of incivility, like those of many other annoying behaviors, can always say their rudeness was unintentional or that
the target misinterpreted it.

The Prevalence of Incivility

Because incivility is subject to misinterpretation, it is difficult to
determine its prevalence. The findings of many surveys, however,
confirm the casual observation that incivility is not only prevalent
but on the rise (Andersson and Pearson, 1999; Pearson, Andersson, and Porath, 2000). Instances of rudeness and uncivil actions
can be seen in business, in schools, in interactions between parents and children, on the highways, in the air, on basketball courts
and baseball diamonds, and on television, particularly during political campaigns.

It has been estimated that up to 13 percent of all words used in
everyday speech are profane (Cameron, 1969; Winters and Duck,
2001). Furthermore, in a survey conducted by *U.S. News and
World Report* (Marks, 1996), researchers found that 89 percent of
Americans thought incivility was a serious problem, and 78 percent believed the problem had worsened in the past ten years. Of
those responding, over 90 percent thought the decline in civility
had contributed to violence, and 84 percent thought it had eroded
people's values. In another survey of Americans' attitudes toward
incivility, 67 percent of respondents blamed incivility on rock mu-

sic, 52 percent blamed it on talk radio, and 34 percent blamed the schools. Interestingly, even though nearly 90 percent of Americans believe incivility is a problem in American life, 99 percent say their own behavior is civil (Kauffman and Burbach, 1998: 15).

Christine Pearson, Lynn Andersson, and Christine Porath (2000) surveyed fourteen hundred workers regarding incivility in the workplace. Of those surveyed, 78 percent said that incivility in the workplace had worsened in the preceding ten years. The study also found that men are worse offenders than women. Twelve percent of the people who experienced rude behavior had quit their jobs to avoid it. Fifty-two percent reported losing work time worrying about rudeness, and 22 percent deliberately decreased their productivity because of it (Gillette, 1999). Thus incivility clearly can have serious consequences.

Is this a new problem? or are we simply finding more and newer ways of being rude? Perhaps we are simply more accepting today of behavior that once was punished. Incivility in one form or another has been around throughout recorded history. In every period and in every culture, people have always uttered forbidden words that today would be called swearing; in the fourteenth century B.C. the Hebrews were commanded, "Thou shalt not take the name of the Lord thy God in vain" (presumably this stricture would hardly have been necessary if people hadn't been bandying his name about in ways not intended as prayerful). In more recent times, the first major writing on civility appeared in the sixteenth century, a book by Erasmus titled *De civilitate morum puerilium* (On civility in children) (Carter, 1998).

Although rudeness and breaches of propriety have been recorded throughout history, Americans seem to be more accepting of such behavior today than they once were, or at least less willing to exert the effort it takes to end it. Children who swore used to have their mouths washed out with soap. Does any parent do that today? Besides, technological advances provide avenues for behaving uncivilly that earlier generations lacked. In many ways, it is simply easier to be rude today than it was in decades past.

Ways in Which Incivility Rears Its Ugly Head

Anyone could generate a list of ways in which people behave rudely or disrespectfully, some more serious than others. What are some general areas in which incivility is a serious problem in our society? My list (far from comprehensive) includes behavior in schools, in political advertising, on talk shows, in general speech, on the Internet, with cell phones, on the road, and in the air. A much more elaborate treatment of some of these manifestations can be found in Stephen Carter's (1998) very interesting book *Civility*.

SCHOOL BEHAVIOR

As Carter has pointed out, schools once operated according to the principle of *in loco parentis:* the school staff acted in place of parents while children were on school premises. The assumption was, of course, that students would respect and obey their teachers in the same way they respected and obeyed their parents. Although this system seems to have worked well for many years, it no longer operates today. In fact, some students today seem to have little or no respect for their teachers. In 1990 an eighth-grade mathematics teacher reported that her students called her names to her face, played radios during class, and threw chairs at one another. A 1991 survey of secondary school teachers revealed that 51 percent had been verbally abused at some time during their teaching careers (Thernstrom, 1999). On the athletic field, baseball players who didn't like the referee's call and football players who didn't like the way the coach looked at them have launched into physical or verbal attacks. Whether students have no respect for any authority figure or reserve their disrespect for teachers and coaches remains to be determined. In either case, the ways some students treat their teachers are truly reprehensible. And some of them seem to be rather proud of themselves. A student of mine named Jack wrote,

When I was a senior in high school I had an English teacher that I liked, but she had been a bitch for the last few weeks. . . . The teacher had given us worksheets for us to use to study for a quiz. When it came time to take the quiz, my best friend and I laid our worksheets on the floor where the information would be visible to copy. During the quiz an extra pen rolled off of my desk and onto the worksheet. When the pen hit the paper, the teacher heard it and saw the worksheet there. When she asked me to turn in the quiz immediately, I said, "What the f*** for?" She told me to leave her class. I told her I wasn't going anywhere. She asked me again and I just rolled my eyes and mumbled, "F*** you, bitch," not knowing she heard me. Instead of me leaving class, she left and got the principal. He then had to come and get me out of class. When he asked me to follow him to the office, I replied, "I have better things to do than talk to you," and walked out of school.

Students do not limit their rude, uncivil, and disrespectful behavior to teachers and school administrators. Students who bully their schoolmates are certainly not being civil. Indeed, lack of concern for the feelings of others lies at the heart of bullying and hurtful teasing.

NEGATIVE CAMPAIGN ADVERTISING

Like many other Americans, I was struck by the large amount of negative campaign advertising during the Republican and Democratic presidential primaries in 2000. On the Republican side, John McCain, claiming that he was going to run a clean campaign with no negative advertising, nevertheless accused George W. Bush of being anti-Catholic because he failed initially to take a stand against Bob Jones University's anti-Catholic policies. Bush, for his part, accused McCain of hypocrisy for accepting financial contributions from corporations while he urged campaign finance reform. On the Democratic side, Americans witnessed frequent sniping between Gore and Bradley and saw Gore often try to take center stage over Bush during the debate. Although negative advertising has been a feature of political campaigns for much of our history, it has become so blatant during recent campaigns that the media have devoted almost as much time to complaints about it as to the candidates. Roughly 75 percent of Americans say that negative political advertising is one of the reasons for the decline in civility in recent years (Marks, 1996).

TALK SHOWS

Although television talk shows may serve a purpose, if mindless entertainment can be said to have a purpose, they have fallen to an all-time low in the topics they air and in the behavior they not only tolerate but encourage, as anyone who has watched Jerry Springer can attest. The behavior of some of the guests on such shows is so uncivilized that sometimes one has to wonder whether the entire show is staged. Not long ago, a TV guide announced that the week's talk shows would discuss "sleeping with partner's beau," "stealing sister's boyfriend," and "wife is a prostitute." On perhaps a slightly more civil note are "moms face off against girlfriends," "past outspoken guests," and "Internet romance liars meet."

Similar incivility can be found on talk radio, at least the kind referred to as "shock radio," the classic example being Howard Stern. Apparently anything goes on the Howard Stern show as he talks about his own and other people's sexual practices, uses profanity, and demeans his guests. Although some people clearly enjoy such radio shows, others find them gross, offensive, degrading, and rude. In short, they find them very uncivil.

SWEARING

Fashions in swearing, as in so much else, have changed over the years. In 1939 Metro-Goldwyn-Mayer, preparing to distribute *Gone with the Wind,* had to wrestle with its corporate soul before it could bring itself to allow Clark Gable to utter Rhett Butler's famous last words to Scarlett O'Hara: "Frankly, my dear, I don't give a damn." Today "damn" hardly counts as swearing, and there are times when swearing seems the only appropriate response. In general, however, swearing is viewed as demeaning and offensive. Were it not, television programs would not have to bleep out profanity. Despite the negative associations with swearing and the generally unfavorable impressions conveyed by people who swear, swearing has become so common that some people do not even notice how often they use profanity. For that matter, fewer and fewer television shows are bleeping out objectionable language, and since the 1950s, when words that we now recognize as profanity cautiously made their way into print intended for the general public (Sampson, 1999), increasing numbers of books and other written materials are filled with swear words.

Even when profanity itself is not the issue, other ways of expressing ourselves can be equally objectionable (Carter, 1998). People speak of "squashing" their opponents; our team is going to "kill" yours. Clearly, there are more respectful ways of conveying the same message than using the language of annihilation.

CYBERINCIVILITY

Cyberspace has provided computer users with yet one more venue for behaving rudely. Whether via e-mail or in on-line chat rooms, many people are more discourteous than they would be if they were speaking face to face. Indeed, the term "flaming" has been adopted to refer to rude and obscene exchanges over the Internet. Most people who use chat rooms disguise their identities. Hiding behind a user name, they make themselves out to be younger, more attractive, or more successful than they really are. Having created a name, they can create a new personality and allow themselves liberties they would otherwise think twice about. Besides, when you can't see the reactions to your words and the other person can't see you, let alone touch you, it's easier to be mean and rude. What's the worst that can happen? The person can do no more than blast you in writing, and you can simply exit the chat room.

Instances of cyberincivility have become so common that many Web masters have established rules for conduct on the Internet—netiquette. It remains to be seen how effective such standards are.

CELLULAR PHONES

More than 76 million Americans were using cell phones by the late 1990s. Using them and liking them are two different things, however. In a survey of 2,628 Americans, 59 percent of respondents said they would rather go to the dentist than sit beside someone who was using a cell phone (Zoroya, 1999). Another survey found that 91 percent of respondents thought it was rude to use a cell phone during a meeting ("Bad-mannered cell phone users," 1999). Cell phone use has become so annoying to Judge Philip Vick in Denton, Texas, that he slaps a fine of a hundred dollars on the owner each time a cell phone rings in his courtroom (National Broadcasting Co., *Today,* Feb. 10, 2000). Some restaurants have resorted to posting signs asking patrons to turn their cell phones off before entering the dining room. And some states are beginning to implement legislation requiring people to pull over to the side of the road when they want to use their cell phones.

ROAD RAGE AND FLYING THE UNFRIENDLY SKIES

One reason people object so strenuously to the use of cell phones in cars is that it interferes with driving and threatens the safety of the other drivers on the road. While people are talking on the phone, they speed up, then slow down, all the while weaving in and out of their lane. Those of us unlucky enough to be driving behind such obnoxious cell phone users often find ourselves becoming increasingly irritated. But if we weren't complaining about cell phone use, some other aspect of other people's driving would set us off. The guy in the pickup is following too closely. And why is that idiot in the left lane if she doesn't want to drive more than 40? The feeling that overtakes you when somebody cuts you off is the beginning of road rage.

A survey by Bridgestone/Firestone revealed that 22 percent of drivers sometimes experience road rage. Nine percent feel road rage "often," another 7 percent every day ("Many drivers confess," 1999). As I was driving down the road recently at rush hour, a very young driver cut me off and then immediately hit the brakes to switch to another lane. I almost plowed into him. When I blew my horn, he gave me the finger. Although some people might consider my horn blowing a breach of propriety, his gesture epitomized to me the uncivil depths to which many in our society today have sunk.

If you think you can escape incivility by forsaking the highway for the friendly skies, think again. Passengers' behavior on airplanes has become increasingly rude in recent years. In 2000, an Air Canada flight from Toronto to Edmonton had to make a stop in Winnipeg because a passenger struck one flight attendant and grabbed another by the head when they refused to serve him any more alcohol. Flight attendants have been bitten and even urinated upon. A male passenger on an international flight defecated on the food cart ("Skies can be treacherous," 2000). Air Canada alone reported eighty instances of air rage in one year ("Unruly passenger," 2000).

At the same time, many airlines could do far more than they do to make passengers feel like respected human beings rather than like cattle to be herded into as little space as possible. We all understand the need for security now, but must the airline prolong the delay by closing one of only two check-in desks just as four large tour buses disgorge passengers? If the plane must wait on the tarmac three hours for takeoff in temperatures close to 100, does the pilot explain the delay and make frequent progress reports, or are you left to suffer in silence? In such a situation does the attendant pass out cups of ice water without being asked, or ignore your request for water and tell you to keep your seat when you try to get it yourself? Do the reading lights work? the ventilators? the headsets? Is the food edible? Does the attendant hit you on the head with a tray or spill coffee on you and fail to apologize? run out of meals before all passengers are served? do nothing about the small child who runs screaming up and down the aisles, grabbing at passengers' peanuts? Air travel doesn't have to be the ordeal it has become. Polite, solicitous attention to passengers' comfort goes a long way toward fending off air rage.

Causes of Incivility

What's happened to cause such a seemingly sharp increase in the prevalence of incivility? Did the counterculture of the 1960s leave such a deep imprint on American society that rudeness and incivility are deemed acceptable? Or has technology advanced to the point where we are no longer required to behave civilly? Have our expectations of people and products risen so high that we are chronically dissatisfied and frustrated and thus more willing to take that frustration out on others? Or has our culture evolved to the point where rudeness has become the norm? In an interesting discussion of incivility, Rowland S. Miller (2001) traces the origins of impropriety to three broad factors: cultural, personal, and situational.

CULTURAL FACTORS

Expectations regarding what is appropriate and expected vary from one generation to the next. Even at a single point in time, cultural variations in appropriate behavior can be found. Sexual behavior that might be deemed highly inappropriate in Western culture is considered normative in other cultures. Several factors contribute to such cultural variations.

Counterculture Shock   A comparison of standards of appropriate behavior in the 1920s and 1960s reveals some critical differences in the two eras. The 1960s were associated with much more freedom and individualism than the 1920s. During the 1960s, people increasingly placed their own interests above those of other people. Concern about giving offense took a backseat to concern about fulfilling one's desires and advancing one's causes.

A focus on one's individual concerns has continued to the present day, at least in Western culture. People are much less involved with others in community and civic organizations than they used to be (Carter, 1998). In the past, when people moved into a neighborhood, they generally intended to put down roots; today they are more transient. Because they move much more often, they see little need to establish connections with others or to be concerned about the needs of those around them. If I want to paint my house purple, why should I care what the neighbors think?

Technology   Behind much of the cultural variation in civility that we observe today is technology. Although most people would agree that technology is generally a good thing, its consequences vis-à-vis civility have been anything but good. The advance of technology has increasingly isolated us from one another. With the invention of television, the time that people used to spend in conversation they began to spend in front of the tube. The telephone, although certainly a useful technological advance, also isolated people. No longer did they have to visit with one another face to face; they could just ring one another up. And if the person on the other end annoyed them, they could simply hang up.

Although not everyone feels comfortable surfing the Web, most people can attest to the benefits the computer age has brought. We can now gain access to information and maintain contacts with others more quickly and more efficiently than ever before. Seems like a good thing, doesn't it? Or does that efficiency come at a cost? When was the last time you sat down and wrote a friend a letter? I don't mean a few paragraphs of e-mail. I mean a real letter that required you to get out the stationery and a pen, write the letter, look up the address, put a stamp on the envelope, and post it. I imagine it may be a little difficult for many of you to think of such a time. What difference does it make, you may ask, whether I write the letter by hand or on the computer? Perhaps none. It is likely, however, that handwritten letters at least appear more heartfelt and sincere than notes that are tapped out quickly and sped on their way when you click "Send." A handwritten letter has a personal quality that is missing from an e-mail. When a relative sent me two pairs of slippers for my twins, my first impulse was to express my thanks in an e-mail. I quickly realized, however, that an e-mail might convey a lack of appreciation. After she had taken the time to go to the store, buy the slippers, wrap them, and send them, an e-mail would appear slapdash. Fortunately, I opted for the respectful thing to do: I picked up the phone and called her, then took pictures of the boys wearing their slippers and enclosed copies in a note to her.

Like the television and telephone, the Internet, however useful, has served to isolate us. Not so many years ago the hours many of us now spend on the Internet were devoted to face-to-face communication. This increasing isolation has not only deprived many adults of needed social contacts but cheated children out of opportunities to develop social skills that would allow them to grow up to be respectful, civil human beings. And as we have noted, the computer age has provided new ways to behave rudely. People are far more willing to say rude, disrespectful things in an e-mail than they are in a letter bearing their signature or in face-to-face conversation. The very anonymity afforded us by telephones and computers appears to make rudeness more likely to occur.

At the same time that technological advances have isolated us, paradoxically they have allowed others to intrude in our lives. Although few of us would want to live without access to a telephone, it does enable telemarketers to reach us at all times of day. It has also made it possible for us to intrude on our friends and relatives. Although we are the ones who have made the intrusion, we feel affronted if the person we have called dares to tell us that it is not a convenient time to talk (Carter, 1998).

Changing Expectations   Technological advances have also contributed to changing expectations, particularly employers' expectations of their employees. With the help of technology, employees are often expected to produce much more than in years past and to do it more quickly. These changes in expectations and in demands both at work and in our personal relationships seem to play a big part in creating incivility. Companies increase pressure on workers. They downsize to save money and expect the same output from the workers who remain. Workplace norms are changing, too. Forty years ago it was understood that in return for good work and loyalty, employees could feel secure in their jobs; today employees have no such assurance. Furthermore, workers are placed in positions for which they have not received adequate training and preparation. Unable to perform effectively, they find themselves barraged by complaints of inefficient service. The stress and anxiety that result are translated into impatience, anger, and poor communication, and ultimately into aggression

(Neuman and Baron, 1997). Indeed, a survey of two hundred employees revealed a direct association between downsizing and increased pressure for productivity on the one hand and aggression on the other (Baron and Neuman, 1996). Dissatisfaction among workers has become so widespread that a Web site is available where employees who must deal with the public can vent their frustrations: http://www.customerssuck.com (Naughton, 2000).

PERSONAL FACTORS

We all differ in more ways than we can count, yet patterns in behavior and response can be identified. What makes some people behave more rudely than others? and why are some people more sensitive than others to uncivil behavior?

Failures in Self-Control   People seem much more willing today to air their grievances and to mouth off to those in positions of authority than they were just a few decades ago. Such behavior has become so common that it often escapes the harsh backlash that invariably followed it in the past. Uncivil behavior such as this may stem from failure at self-control, or, as social psychologists refer to it, breakdown in self-regulation. Social psychologists have found that "the majority of contemporary social and personal problems afflicting Western society contained some significant element of self-regulation failure" (Dale and Baumeister, 1999: 139–40).

People are often unwilling to monitor their behavior and unwilling to put forth an effort to control their impulses. In a frustrating situation, such as being cut off by another driver, our first impulse is often to swear at the driver or make an obscene gesture or, at minimum, lean on the horn. In fact, it takes conscious effort to inhibit such impulses. If our desire to respond to rudeness with rudeness is intense or if our ability to control our impulses is weak, perhaps because our day has already supplied our full quota of frustrations, we may make no effort to control our behavior. The first time we let loose in this way, the situation is often minor. Having failed once to control a particular behavior, however, we become increasingly likely to give up future efforts at self-control, and the situation escalates as our self-control deteriorates.

Lack of Effort Some people behave badly simply because they don't care about their society's rules of civil behavior or are unwilling to make the effort required to behave civilly. Think of a time when you have arrived home exhausted after a long, frustrating day, only to be nagged about your share of chores left undone—dishes in the sink, coffee grounds on the kitchen floor. If you could bring yourself to grab the broom and say, "Sorry, hon, I'll do all the dishes after dinner," all would probably be well. But the effort to behave civilly is often more than we can muster, so we respond rudely and the battle is on. It often requires effort to stop ourselves from making critical, biting remarks to our significant other. We are far more likely to criticize our spouse's overboiled spaghetti than the equally overcooked asparagus served by a friend who has invited us to dinner. We exert much less effort to control our impulses with our spouse than with other people.

Ignorance Some people behave rudely because they simply don't understand the rules of appropriate behavior in the context in which they find themselves. People who have never before attended a formal dinner party, for example, are quite likely to do or say something the other guests consider improper. They are not unwilling to behave courteously, they simply don't know what is expected of them.

The relation between ignorance and incivility becomes particularly prominent when people visit other countries. Unaware of the behavior considered appropriate in a country strange to them, people may be guilty of serious breaches of propriety. People in Western societies value personal space, for example, much more highly than Middle Easterners. We keep what we consider an appropriate distance between us when we talk; Middle Easterners stand so close together that they can feel each other's breath. To an American speaking with a Syrian, say, the Syrian appears extremely pushy, literally in your face; the American feels crowded and uncomfortable. To the Syrian the American seems rude and standoffish as he keeps backing away.

Personality   Some people are just more inclined to be uncivil than others. They either care nothing about the effect of their behavior on other people or they lack conscientiousness in following the rules of appropriate behavior. Many of the annoying behaviors we have been considering, such as complaining and teasing, could be considered rude and uncivil. Some people complain or tease for the sole purpose of annoying and hurting other people.

Moreover, personality may make some people more ready to perceive another person's behavior as annoying. Someone who is very outgoing, for example, may view someone who is shy and withdrawn as rude and standoffish (Miller, 2001). Similarly, men and women whose behavior fails to accord with their society's gender stereotypes may be perceived as disrespectful. Thus a man who fails to open a door for a woman or a woman who fails to thank the man who opened the door may be perceived as rude. Yet because cultural norms vary from place to place and are constantly changing, it is often difficult to know what sort of behavior will be considered appropriate in a particular situation.

Are men or women more likely to break the rules of propriety? The types of rude behaviors that immediately come to mind are typically those associated with men. Part of the reason harks back to the stereotypical expectations of men and women. When a man belches, he's—well, just being a guy. A belch from a woman is viewed as much more distasteful. In addition, traditionally men have held more social power than women, power that gives them greater freedom to behave "inappropriately." Norms are changing, though, and more and more women are adopting inappropriate behaviors once considered appropriate only for men. Although men typically swear twice as often as women (Jay, 1992), the frequency with which women swear has increased (Winters and Duck, 2001). This is not to say, however, that once women adopt a behavior, it becomes acceptable. Swearing is typically viewed as inappropriate no matter who does it (Winters and Duck, 2001).

SITUATIONAL FACTORS

Among the situational factors that lead to incivility are changes in the norms of behavior, so that what once was considered absolutely unacceptable now appears less so, and accidental factors that override the rules of acceptable behavior. But perhaps the greatest trigger of incivility is incivility itself. As instances of incivility increase, a culture of incivility is created.

Incivility Another person's rudeness or inconsiderateness makes most people angry, or at minimum puts them in a bad mood. Although they could choose to do nothing, their immediate impulse may be to retaliate. Some people, when they are tailgated on the highway, let the offenders pass and then give them a taste of their own medicine by riding their tail. Although they must know the practice is highly unsafe, their anger is somehow relieved.

The strength of an impulse to seek revenge for rudeness depends on how emotionally reactive one tends to be and on the mood one is in at the time. People who wear their emotions on their sleeves are likely to respond to rudeness with rudeness. Similarly, for people who have had a bad day, gratuitous rudeness may simply be the straw that breaks the camel's back, and they lash out.

Incivility can breed incivility in yet another way. Even if people do not retaliate with rudeness, exposure to incivility may increase the likelihood that they will behave uncivilly at some future time. If the way I behave is then imitated by someone who has witnessed it, social psychologists would say that I had modeled that behavior. Children in particular are highly susceptible to modeling. Although television executives claim that profanity and violence on network television simply mirror current societal trends (Leo, 1996), it may also be true that people, especially children, who watch incivility on television become ruder themselves as a result. Closer to home, children imitate the rude behaviors of their parents, subordinates imitate the poor manners of their superiors, and students mirror the actions of their teachers. As John Leo (1996) has noted, "Partly because the anything-goes ethic is now so strong, corporations are more willing to get attention through aggressive, assaultive advertising. They understand that in-your-face messages that shred social norms can move the merchandise by playing to the current sour, antisocial mood. Thus, the rapid spread of ads urging us to break all of the rules or just make up our own" (73). Witnessing other people's incivility not only lowers one's own inhibitions but also increases feelings of surliness and hostility, which themselves can trigger uncivil behavior.

The role played by modeling in incivility depends in part on how clear the rules of behavior are in a particular situation. When the rules of appropriate behavior are clearly laid out, as they are in religious services, rude or discourteous behavior is unlikely to be imitated. A person who stands up in the middle of a sermon and begins to shout at the minister will in all likelihood be removed from the premises and her behavior attributed to some mental disturbance. If someone stands up at a rock concert and shouts at the musicians, however, the behavior will probably be imitated.

Changing Norms Norms, as Rowland Miller (2001) notes, evolve: views of what is appropriate change over time. Grooming routines that dating couples would not dream of letting their partners witness—she shaving her legs, he clipping hairs in his nostrils—no longer require privacy after the relationship has developed. The cliché that the person you marry is not the same person you dated can be attributed largely to the change in norms. While you're dating, you're generally on your best behavior. After you marry, you relax and feel comfortable "being yourself." What was once taboo is now permissible.

Allowable Offenses When circumstances are beyond our control or we are faced with an emergency, certain breaches of propriety are allowed and perhaps even considered appropriate in the circumstances. Thus a husband driving over the speed limit to get his wife to the hospital because she is in labor is excused because of the circumstances.

The Consequences of Incivility

When people behave rudely toward you, how do you feel? Irritated? Angry? Do you feel that people are deliberately trying to offend you or that they are unaware of the effects of their behavior? Does it matter? Would your reaction be different if you knew that they were simply unaware of their impropriety? What are the consequences of incivility to businesses and relationships? Does incivility have legal implications?

Incivility results in a lack of communication, a lack of respect, negative feelings, and a decline in productivity (Windsor, 1999). Thus incivility clearly has negative consequences for businesses.

Eticon, an etiquette consulting firm in Columbia, South Carolina, conducted a survey on workplace rudeness. Roughly 80 percent of the 1,281 respondents said that workplace rudeness had increased in recent years. Queried about their reactions to rudeness by a salesperson, 58 percent said they would take their business elsewhere, 42 percent said they would file a formal complaint, and 25 percent said they would talk with the salesperson's supervisor (Bass, 1999).

In personal relationships, too, incivility undermines communication and respect and arouses negative feelings. Although we tend to be ruder and more uncivil to those we love than we are to total strangers, most of us expect our romantic partners and friends to treat us with respect and decency. When they don't, particularly if their lack of respect continues over a period of time, we may become so disillusioned with the relationship that we decide to end it.

Some breaches of propriety even lead to legal action. A taxi driver in Hong Kong, for example, was charged with uncivil behavior for swearing at a passenger who took only a short cab ride ("Taxi driver's swearing," 1999). A man who swore after he fell out of a canoe and was overheard by a couple and their child faced criminal prosecution for violating a 102-year-old Michigan law forbidding the use of profanity in the presence of women and children (ABC, *Nightline*, June 11, 1999). Companies are warning their employees that profanity and sexist or racist jokes create a hostile work environment and make them liable to charges of harassment.

Perhaps even more serious are acts of aggression that stem from acts of incivility. When incivility breeds more incivility, it can spiral out of control and explode in violence. Research has shown incivility to be correlated with crime (Andersson and Pearson, 1999; Goldstein, 1994), including murder and domestic violence.

This Is Incivility?

Some attempts to breed civility may be misguided, focusing on "offenses" that few people recognize rather than on real problems that deserve attention. In attempts to increase civility in the workplace, for example, some companies now offer classes in business etiquette. Employees are taught, among other things, to wear their name tags on the right side and to place their napkins on their chairs rather than on the table when they get up from the table (Goetz, 1999). Does it really matter what side of your body your name tag is on? Is it really inappropriate to place your napkin on the table? Apparently some people think so.

At the other extreme is the airline passenger who defecated on the food cart. Is that behavior appropriate? Certainly not. Rude? Extremely. But is it just your basic incivility, or does it cross the line into pathology? Since most of us cannot imagine choosing that way to demonstrate our anger or frustration, it seems to me inappropriate to classify it as simple incivility; surely such behavior is symptomatic of an underlying psychological disturbance.

Decreasing Rudeness

Methods of decreasing rudeness and increasing civility depend in part on who the culprits are. Parents can discipline a child who sticks his tongue out at a visitor but a subordinate can hardly discipline a rude superior. Some measures, however, may be applied to incivility wherever it may be found. One means of correcting rudeness is to model appropriate behavior. Parents who provide models of rudeness, incivility, or bad manners will almost inevitably have rude children. A CEO who speaks caustically to underlings is modeling such behavior as appropriate for middle managers. The reverse behavior is equally effective. Parents and managers who model civil, courteous behavior and adopt a zero-tolerance policy for uncivil behavior will have children and employees who also behave civilly.

Other measures can be employed to reduce the incidence of rudeness or prevent it from escalating into violence. The "broken window" concept (if the window is broken, it's already too late) is based on the idea that "if you give 'em an inch, they'll take a mile." When children or adults are allowed to get away with seemingly minor instances of rudeness or disrespect, manifestations of incivility will increase over time (Thernstrom, 1999). Thus stopping incivility before it escalates will obviously reduce its frequency.

Some schools are implementing programs analogous to the business etiquette classes introduced in business firms. In Omaha, Nebraska, a life skills program is designed to teach civility and responsibility to students beginning in elementary school. In addition, school administrators have implemented classroom management training programs so that breaches of propriety can be dealt with immediately. Other school systems have adopted zero-tolerance policies in regard to profanity and disrespect. Students who violate the policy are suspended (Stover, 1999).

Incivility and rudeness would disappear if people simply followed the Golden Rule—do unto others as you would have them do unto you. To follow the Golden Rule effectively, however, one must consider other people's perspectives. That is what is so difficult, particularly in the individualistic, fast-paced society in which we now live. In instances in which the Golden Rule does not apply, as with allowable offenses, the offenders should attempt to acknowledge or make reparations for their objectionable behavior. A simple apology can go a long way toward minimizing negative reactions to offensive behavior.

Reducing incivility does not require us to suppress our own needs and opinions altogether. It requires only that we behave toward others and express our opinions with respect. Just as you should be willing to listen respectfully to others who disagree with you, so they should be willing to listen to you with equal respect when your opinions differ from theirs.

Just as incivility breeds incivility, civility breeds civility. The more we model respectful behavior, the more others will respond to that behavior in kind. As Carter (1998) notes, however, in order to practice civility successfully, people must be willing to suspend their own needs long enough to factor in the needs and feelings of other people. Thus, even though we may be temporarily inconvenienced by pulling off to the side of the road when we feel it necessary to use our cellular phones, the best interests of everyone on the highway will be better served. Only then will true civility be practiced.

If we can't manage to decrease the incidence of incivility, we can at least learn to control the effect that rudeness and disrespect have on us. We can respond with anger less often if we distinguish between true impositions or violations of expectations, to which anger may be a justifiable response (neighbor at your door with scowling toddler in tow: "I know you won't mind if I leave Ashley with you for a couple of hours while I dash to get my hair done, Mr. Freddie simply won't let me bring her with me") and breaches of propriety that really, in the grand scheme of things, don't matter and can be laughed off (same neighbor, same toddler, now smiling winsomely: "Ashley's nursery school is holding a white elephant sale, and I remembered that hideous lamp in your den"). In the latter case, responding with anger will accomplish nothing more than ruining your day.

A second way to dispel the anger-arousing effects of rudeness is to cast obnoxious behavior in a more positive light. Notice that we usually find it easier to let another person's incivility pass without comment when our day is otherwise going well than when we are in a foul mood. If everyone seems to be obnoxious and getting on your nerves, perhaps the best thing to do is to chalk it up to a bad day and let it go.

If these suggestions are followed, can incivility be decreased? Can we know again the greater degree of civility our society once enjoyed? If we remember that no society has ever been entirely free of incivility, yes, we can. The key difference between then and now is that in times long gone people depended on one another to a much greater extent than they do today. Without the technology that makes life easier for us in so many ways, they were often forced to inhibit their impulses for the common good and for their own. A farm woman couldn't expect her neighbors to pitch in and help get the hay in the barn before the storm broke if she weren't on good terms with them, despite their annoying idiosyncrasies; her husband couldn't have depended on his neighbors to help him build that barn if his neighbors hadn't known they could depend on him when they needed help, whether it was convenient for him or not. If today we took equal care to nourish good feelings, then yes, we could experience the civility that smoothed social life in years past, despite the lapses in civility that would inevitably occur.

6

• • • • • • • •

Excessive Worry and
Reassurance-Seeking

Some people seem to worry most of the time, others only sporadically, but we all know what it is to worry. We may not worry about the same things that Rick did, but we can understand the anxiety that overwhelmed him and the relief he felt when his fears proved to be unfounded:

> I recently took an HIV test. You have to wait seven to ten days for the results, and I worried the entire time. I thought of every risky thing I had ever done. I divided all my sex partners into categories (low risk and high risk). I was so scared I would have to tell my parents and my current partner I had tested positive. It was so scary. To make myself feel better, I tried not to think about it. I also prayed a lot. My friends were wonderful. They kept telling me I was fine, and they assured me that even if I weren't, they would be there for me. Finally I got my results back and they were negative. I felt like a million pounds of worry had been lifted from me.

At first blush, worry may appear to be troublesome only to the worrier. Unfortunately, the distress caused by worry can reach beyond the worrier to other people. Edward Hallowell (1997) noted the impact of worry on relationships when he wrote that "toxic worry is like an acid that burns away the cables that connect an individual" (271). It's not the worry itself that's bothersome to other people, it's the behaviors that accompany it.

One of the most troublesome of these behaviors is excessive seeking of reassurance. Worriers need reassurance, and when they implore us to reassure them in ways great and small, over and over and over, we become fed up. We all need reassurance from time to time, but enough is enough. Anyone who has been around a chronic worrier for any length of time knows how frustrating this excessive reassurance-seeking can be. Refusal to be concerned about problems that need to be faced is frustrating too, but constant seeking of reassurance has probably broken up at least as many relationships as turning a blind eye ever did.

Worry

We have all known chronic worriers. They can make a mountain out of a molehill. Such comforting old saws as "Most of the things you worry about never happen" and "Worry is interest paid on trouble before it's due" are meaningless to chronic worriers. Unable to turn off their worry, they must seek assurance from others.

Worry is often accompanied by fear or anxiety. Indeed, excessive worry is the key characteristic of a psychological disorder known as generalized anxiety disorder (American Psychiatric Association, 1994). People with generalized anxiety disorder worry excessively and find it very difficult to control their worry. Most people with generalized anxiety disorder appear to be genetically predisposed to worry excessively. They tend to be high-strung, and frequently at least one other family member is known as a chronic worrier. This biological predisposition is what distinguishes worry from the other annoying behaviors discussed here, such as complaining and teasing. Although some personality traits may pre-

---

Are You a Worrywart?

The Penn State Worry Questionnaire measures people's tendency to worry regardless of the situation in which they find themselves. To assess your propensity to worry, complete the scale on pg. 128.

After you have indicated a score for each item, reverse your scores for the items marked "(R)." In other words, change a 5 to 1, a 4 to 2, a 2 to 4, and a 1 to 5; 3 remains 3. Once you have made these changes, add up your scores. The higher your total score, the more of a worrier you are.

---

dispose someone to complain or tease excessively, these behaviors are not prewired in the same way that worry often is (Hallowell, 1997).

Although worry often has a genetic basis, it may also be triggered solely by life experiences. "Many people who worry too much do so out of some kind of broken trust or loss of faith," writes Hallowell (1997: 19). "If you suffer injustice in a major way at the wrong time you may never be the same. You may worry forever after." You may worry so that you don't have to feel the pain associated with past hurts and betrayals. Our ability to focus attention on more than one thing at a time is extremely limited. If you channel all your attention toward something that worries you, you'll have little capacity left to focus on the things that hurt you in the past. In essence, you are trading one type of distress for another.

Here we find one of the ironies in the relationship between worry and reassurance-seeking: people whose worry stems from broken trust often turn to other people in search of reassurance. It would seem that their lack of faith in others would lead them

Table 6.1. Penn State Worry Questionnaire

Using the following scale, indicate how characteristic of you each of the items below is:

1 = Not at all characteristic of me
2 = Somewhat characteristic of me
3 = Moderately characteristic of me
4 = Very characteristic of me
5 = Extremely characteristic of me

_____ 1. If I don't have enough time to do everything, I don't worry about it. (R)

_____ 2. My worries overwhelm me.

_____ 3. I don't tend to worry about things. (R)

_____ 4. Many situations make me worry.

_____ 5. I know I shouldn't worry about things, but I just can't help it.

_____ 6. When I'm under pressure, I worry a lot.

_____ 7. I am always worrying about something.

_____ 8. I find it easy to dismiss worrisome thoughts. (R)

_____ 9. As soon as I finish one task, I start to worry about everything else I have to do.

_____ 10. I never worry about anything. (R)

_____ 11. When there is nothing more I can do about a concern, I don't worry about it anymore. (R)

_____ 12. I've been a worrier all my life.

_____ 13. I notice that I have been worrying about things.

_____ 14. Once I start worrying, I can't stop.

_____ 15. I worry all the time.

_____ 16. I worry about projects until they are all done.

Source: Reprinted from *Behavior Research and Therapy, 28*, Meyer, Miller, Metzger, and Borkovec, "Development and Validation of the Penn State Worry Questionnaire," 487–95, copyright © 1990, with permission from Elsevier Science.

to doubt any reassurance they might receive. And there's the rub. In fact, excessive worriers *do* doubt the reassurances that others offer them. And it is this doubt, in conjunction with the persistence with which worriers seek reassurance, that makes worrying so annoying.

WHAT DO PEOPLE WORRY ABOUT?

When I conducted a survey to gain some insight into the broad categories of issues that cause people the most concern, I found that people worry primarily about three things: relationships, their health, and the future.

Relationships arouse a tremendous amount of worry. Some of my respondents worried about the whereabouts of their significant others (Why haven't I heard from him?); others expressed concern about the current state of their relationships (If I accept the invitation to Washington, will he get mad? Is she going to find out what I was really doing last weekend?). Still others worried about losing important relationships, as Kate did:

> I was dating a guy very seriously (we were talking about marriage) and there was something in my past that I felt he probably needed to know. I knew this particular thing was going to hurt him, and I was afraid it would make him change the way he felt about me. It worried me sick! I mean I couldn't eat, I couldn't sleep. It consumed my thoughts, and I hated myself for doing it. At one point, I tried to tell myself it was in the past and it needed to stay there, that there was no need to hurt him. I did a pretty good job for a while, but I never convinced myself and I still worried like crazy. I sought others people's advice—should I tell him about this even though it would hurt him? Some said yes and some said no. None of them made me feel better, but I kept asking people to try to make myself feel better. Still I worried and realized I never would feel better until this wall between us came down, until I told him what happened. So I sat down and told him. I was right—it killed him. But after we both calmed down, he said we would work through this thing together and he had forgiven me. From that day on, I haven't worried about it any more.

Health was another big focus of worry. Some women worried that they might be pregnant; some men worried that an injury they had suffered would never heal properly. Rick, who checked his HIV status, wasn't the only one who worried about the results of a physical test. Dolores worried that she might have breast cancer:

> They found a suspicious lump in my breast and scheduled two different mammograms to get a closer look. I had to wait about six weeks between them so they could see if the lump grew or changed. I worried it was cancer. I tried to convince myself that it was nothing because I scored low on the risk scale. I talked to my sisters and they reassured me that no one in our family had had breast cancer, although two of my sisters had had lumps. When the lump moved before the second mammogram, I was very relieved. They assured me it was nothing to worry about then.

Many of our respondents worried about the future. Because we were surveying college students, many of them worried about upcoming tests, graduating on time, getting into graduate school, getting a job. Margo worried about losing her parents:

> I remember when I was little, about five or so, lying in my bed at night and sobbing as I listened to the voices of my parents in the other room. I would do this several nights a week, but no one ever knew. I was absolutely terrified that my parents were going to die and I would be left alone. I never sought reassurance during these episodes. I would simply cry myself to sleep. I just couldn't and didn't want to be without my parents. As I reflect upon it now, I realize that I am still fearful and worried that my parents will die and I will lose a bond never to be found again. I get reassurance now by spending time with them and learning as much as I can. I guess this has not resolved itself and I don't think it ever will. How could it?

Some worries are more generalized and tend to be the most dangerous for the worrier because they are more likely to have a harmful effect on self-esteem and relationships, as we see in Sandy's comments: "I was and am still worried about flunking out of school, disappointing my family, and failing as a parent. My child always makes me feel better. I talked about it to someone with whom I felt comfortable. It hasn't been resolved and perhaps never will be because there will always be this feeling of worthlessness and failure, even if I feel I can console myself for a little while."

FUNCTIONS OF WORRY

Thomas Borkovec (1994) has identified five functions that worry may serve. All five allow people to avoid a threatening situation or outcome, at least in their own minds. First is what Borkovec refers to as the "superstitious avoidance of catastrophe": some people believe that if they worry about something they fear, it will be less likely to happen. Since most of the things we worry about never happen anyway, their belief is reinforced. When the thing they fear doesn't happen, they are convinced that they fended it off by their clever strategy of worrying about it.

Second, worry may in fact allow us to avoid something we fear. If my car has been giving me trouble and I worry that it will break down before I have time to take it to a mechanic, my worry may cause me to take the bus to work or catch a ride with someone else. Because I worried, I avoided getting stuck in rush-hour traffic in a car that wouldn't run.

Third, because we have limited capacity to attend to more than one thing at a time, if we worry about little things, we may avoid worrying about bigger things. So you may worry about when you will get all your Christmas shopping done in order to prevent yourself from worrying about your sister's tottering marriage or your father's forced retirement.

Fourth, worrying about something may actually prepare you to cope with the event if it does occur. When we worry about something, we often rehearse in our minds the best way to react if it happens. Thus we have prepared ourselves to deal with it when and if it does happen.

Finally, worry can serve as a motivator, prompting us to get done what needs to be done. If you worry about getting the guest room in shape before your mother-in-law's upcoming visit, you'll get started on the job instead of procrastinating until she's at the door.

Reassurance-Seeking

People seek reassurance when they feel insecure, worried, or anxious. Al had overcome a problem that troubled him, but still he wanted to be reassured that the problem was truly gone: "I had a problem with the way I perceived my appearance. I was very overweight at one time, and very self-conscious. I began to work out and lost weight. I was constantly seeking reassurance from my peers and my family. I always felt that I looked bad, and that I needed that reassurance to feel better. I was very dependent upon my girlfriend at the time. I always had to have her reassurance about my weight."

Are You an Excessive Reassurance-Seeker?

Your tendency to seek reassurance can be measured. The scale most frequently used to measure individual differences in reassurance-seeking was developed by Thomas Joiner, Jr., a clinical psychologist at Florida State University.

After you've answered the questions, following the directions provided, add up your scores. The higher your score, the greater your tendency to seek reassurance.

Table 6.2. Reassurance-Seeking Scale

Answer each of the questions below, using the following scale:

1 = No, not at all   5 = Yes, somewhat
2 = No, hardly ever   6 = Yes, quite often
3 = Not really   7 = Yes, *very* often
4 = I'm not sure

_____ 1. In general, do you find yourself often asking the people you feel close to how they *truly* feel about you?

_____ 2. In general, do you frequently seek reassurance from people you feel close to as to whether they *really* care about you?

_____ 3. In general, do the people you feel close to sometimes become irritated with you for seeking reassurance from them about whether they *really* care about you?

_____ 4. In general, do the people you feel close to sometimes get fed up with you for seeking reassurance from them about whether they *really* care about you?

Source: Reproduced by kind permission of Dr. Thomas Joiner, Jr.

All of us seek reassurance from other people from time to time. We may ask our friends if we look okay or if they really think our new haircut is right for us. We seek reassurance from our teachers that our grades are okay or from our boss that our job performance is satisfactory. No matter how confident or self-assured we are, we all have blips of self-doubt that a reassuring word from another person can quickly allay. Thus reassurance-seeking per se is very common and often functional. It becomes a problem only when it is excessive, and then its usefulness is slight and temporary. "Reassurance is the safest, least expensive Band-Aid for worry that we have," writes Edward Hallowell (1997: 267), "but it is only a Band-Aid and does not solve any underlying problems."

Some people are by nature more clingy and dependent than others. Whereas some people rarely seem to need confirmation that they are acceptable and even likable, others are constantly seeking out others' approval. People whose self-esteem is low are particularly likely to rely on the reassurances of others to make them feel better about themselves.

Two characteristics seem to be predictors of who is likely to seek reassurance to excess: dependency and sensitivity to rejection.

DEPENDENCY

A dependent person has been described as "a cooperative, compliant individual who looks to other people for nurturance, protection, and support, preferring to seek the advice and guidance of others rather than acting according to his [or her] own beliefs and inclinations" (Bornstein et al., 1993: 262). People who are dependent ask for help more often than those who are not. This difference can be noted even in children: some seek help and reassurance from their teachers more than others. Anyone who has interacted frequently with a dependent person knows how tiring and wearing it can be. It seems that no matter what you say, the dependent person continues to seek reassurance from you about one thing or another.

SENSITIVITY TO REJECTION

People vary in their sensitivity to signs that other people reject them. Whereas some people seem not to notice, or at least not to care, other people become very distressed at even the slightest hint that someone may be rejecting them. These people are so sensitive to signs of rejection that they may see rejection when in fact none was intended. In one study (Downey and Feldman, 1996), people high in rejection sensitivity were told that another person no longer wanted to associate with them. No explanation for why the person wanted to stop associating with them was provided. Subjects high in rejection sensitivity interpreted the other person's behavior as intentional rejection; no other conceivable explanation occurred to them.

Naturally enough, people high in rejection sensitivity are prone to depression (Ayduk, Downey, and Kim, 2001). In an effort to stave off depression, they constantly seek reassurance that others are not really rejecting them. This behavior becomes so tiresome that it leads to the very rejection they feared.

To identify people who are high in rejection sensitivity, Geraldine Downey and Scott Feldman (1996) created a Rejection Sensitivity Questionnaire. Respondents are presented with eighteen hypothetical situations in which they might expect rejection and are asked how likely they think they are to be rejected in each situation and how concerned they are about the outcome. Representative situations include: "You ask someone in one of your classes to coffee"; "You ask your parents to come to an occasion important to you."

Although people clearly vary in their tendency to seek reassurance, situations can also induce dependency and excessive reassurance-seeking, particularly situations that lead one to feel depressed. Lucy described one such situation:

My husband's grandmother was having surgery. It was supposed to be a simple procedure, but something went wrong and she got very sick. Her lungs started to fail. She had an up-and-down week. Just when they thought she was getting better, she died. She was only fifty-seven. Even before she died my husband had a hard time with the situation. He became very clingy. He just wanted me to be beside him and tell him that everything would be okay. He was constantly holding my hand or touching me so he would know I was there. He didn't want to talk about it much, but he would want me to hug him. He always wanted me to go to the hospital with him, to be with him in his grandmother's room. It was as if I were some security blanket for him.

As Lucy so perceptively noted, reassurance does work much like a security blanket, wrapping the needy one in warmth and safety. If her husband had also been a chronic worrier, however, reassurance would not have provided the security he craved. Worriers who do not respond well to offers of reassurance are typically those who are also depressed. Indeed, their worry is really just a cover for their depression.

Thomas Joiner, Jr., studied excessive reassurance-seeking as an aspect of what he calls depressotypic behavior. Depression itself is not particularly annoying. It is only when depression leads to depressotypic behavior, such as excessive reassurance-seeking, that it becomes a problem for other people. As Katz and Joiner (2001) have written, "Depressotypic behaviors communicate several types of aversive messages. They may communicate that the partner is implicated in the development of the problem . . . or that the relationship is no longer satisfying and rewarding. . . . Depressotypic behaviors may overwhelm relationship partners with demands, whether implicit or stated, for help" (118).

By constantly seeking reassurance, worriers are also conveying to their friends and relationship partners that they do not trust the reassurance they are being offered. According to Bill Swann and Jennifer Bosson (1999), "When depressed persons indicate that they are unconvinced by their partner's expressions of love and reassurance, their partners receive the implicit message that they are not credible sources of feedback. . . . Insofar as nondepressed partners think of themselves as honest, trustworthy, and reliable . . . , the unabated incredulity of depressed persons will represent a direct challenge to their beliefs about themselves" (302).

Excessive reassurance-seekers place themselves and those from whom they are seeking reassurance in a tough spot (Hallowell, 1997). If they simply want reassurance, the request needs to be explicit—"Tell me you still love me." If they want the truth rather than simply what they'd like to hear, the request becomes "Do you still love me?"

Perhaps for this reason, some reassurance-seekers couch their requests in ways that deprive them of the very reassurance they are seeking. A woman who fears she has gained weight, for example, may ask her husband, "Do I look okay in this dress?" What she wants to hear is that she looks beautiful, as she always does, but what she hears is "Sure, you look okay." Her dissatisfaction at a response that falls so far short of her hopes may set up a round of reassurance-seeking: "Just okay? I just look *okay?*" How is he to respond to that? He answered her original question but clearly not in a way that provided the reassurance she desired. Nothing he says is likely to mollify her now.

Consequences of Excessive Reassurance-Seeking

One problem with excessive reassurance-seeking is that at first another person's dependence on us can be flattering, as Jennifer noted:

> I have had many boyfriends who have been pretty dependent on me but one sticks out in particular. This problem started off to be sort of flattering. It would make me feel good when I knew I was needed so much. But when it began to get worse and I felt like I couldn't go anywhere without him, it was not flattering at all. It felt like I could never have any kind of personal space. It was very hard for me to explain to him that this was the reason we were breaking up. When we finally did break up, it was like I had my whole life back.

We all want to feel needed and few of us mind another person's occasional dependence on us. It makes us feel useful and desired. In time, however, the reassurance-seeking ceases to be flattering and becomes annoying and draining, as Darren discovered: "I became friends with a girl I met at work. At first she seemed really nice and outgoing, but as time went on, things changed. It was a slow process, but eventually she couldn't do anything without me. I started to feel suffocated." In spite of their initial flattering qualities, worry and excessive reassurance-seeking lead to feelings of ineffectiveness, depression, rejection, and dysphoria.

FEELINGS OF INEFFECTIVENESS

When someone keeps on begging for reassurance after you have already offered it again and again, you may be forgiven for feeling that your efforts to reassure him are not very effective. You may well decide not to provide any more reassurance, since it doesn't seem to matter anyway. The depressed person then sinks further into depression, convinced that you don't love him after all (Swann and Bosson, 1999).

This is a particular problem when the person seeking reassurance is a narcissist. Narcissists typically want you to confirm, again and again, that they are as good and as worthy as they think they are. All the reassurance in the world is unlikely to provide the support the narcissist wants.

THE CONTAGION OF DEPRESSION

Depression can be contagious (Katz, Beach, and Joiner, 1999). The feeling of "What's the use?" that overwhelms us after repeated attempts to reassure a depressed person may lead us into depression too. James Coyne and his colleagues (1987) found that more than 40 percent of the persons they surveyed who lived with a depressed person reported clinical symptoms of depression themselves, compared to 17 percent of those whose roommates were not depressed.

REJECTION

Perhaps in an effort to preserve their own mental equilibrium, reassurance providers frequently end up rejecting the reassurance seeker. College students with same-sex roommates were more likely to reject roommates who were depressed *and* in excessive need of reassurance than roommates who were not depressed and seldom or never sought reassurance (Joiner and Metalsky, 1995). Husbands whose wives were depressed and sought reassurance to excess were more dissatisfied in their relationships than husbands whose wives did not fit this description (Katz and Beach, 1997; see also Katz and Joiner, 2001). Note here that it is not simply depressed people who are being rejected but depressed people who seek constant reassurance. Many relationships have ended because one partner simply tires of offering reassurance to the other, tires of coping with persistent clinginess and dependency.

DYSPHORIA

Not all the consequences of excessive reassurance-seeking are interpersonal. Indeed, reassurance-seekers themselves can experience a host of negative personal consequences, most of which can be placed under the heading of dysphoria, or negative emotion. Because they are highly sensitive to rejection, excessive reassurance-seekers expect to be rejected. Thus they may bring about the very rejection they so fear, with resultant dysphoria. When they believe they have every reason to expect support, the hurt of rejection can be even sharper, as Meg discovered: "When my grandmother died, I became very needy and dependent on my older brother. He had known my grandmother longer but I was closer to her. After the funeral, I wouldn't leave his side. For close to a month I called him every day to find out all I could about my grandmother. After a while, we argued when he said I was destroying his personal life. For three months, I wouldn't speak to him. He had severely hurt me."

Jody, too, became angry when the person she clung to failed to provide the reassurance she wanted:

> I was very clingy with my best friend a couple of years ago. I was in a bad car accident, and afterward I fell into depression. I clung to my best friend because she was all I had, and if I lost her as my best friend, I would have felt completely hopeless. I wanted to spend all my free time with her, and I tried to, but she also had other people in her life, like her boyfriend. I got offended and hurt when she wanted to spend time with people other than me, and we fought about it. Eventually my depression ended, and I didn't feel I had to cling to her anymore as a source of happiness.

Failure to get the desired reassurance may lead worriers to worry more than ever. Because they cannot stop worrying despite other people's best efforts to help them, they may worry, as indeed they should, that other people will withdraw from them. The more they worry about being rejected, the more likely it is that their friends will reject them. Worrying of this sort is a self-fulfilling prophecy.

Finally, chronic worriers may come to fear that there is something wrong with them. Other people don't seem to worry like this, so what's wrong with them that they can't stop worrying? Why can't they at least wait until something happens that they really need to worry about? And, in fact, other people may be thinking the same thing. "What's wrong with you?" they say. Whether the question occurs first to the worrier or to someone else, the effect on the worrier's self-esteem is the same.

What to Do

One reason that reassurance may not be the cure-all that worriers hope for is that a single worry can branch out along many lines, or, in the words of Edward Hallowell (1997), "can kindle a whole bonfire of anxiety" (72). If I worry that my children may pick up a virus at daycare, I then can't help thinking about all the other things that might happen to them there. Can I be absolutely sure they'll be well cared for and happy? What if some other child hits them? What if they hit some other child? Oh, but they wouldn't— would they? What if some demented person breaks in with a gun and kidnaps my children? What if . . . Well, you get the idea. Not only do I feel the need to call the daycare provider now, but any reassurance I get will be unlikely to banish all my worries. Although someone can remind me how unlikely it is that my children will be kidnapped, no one can tell me with the same degree of confidence that they will not get sick at daycare.

Worries need to be nipped in the bud before they can blossom and send out shoots. If I hadn't worried about my children at daycare in the first place, or at least not excessively, none of the other worries would have gotten started. Yet somehow I feel that if I worry about it, then nothing bad will happen. After all, don't they say that most of the things you worry about never happen? If I didn't worry about things almost as if to prevent them from happening, then I might worry that I wasn't showing the proper concern, and here we go again.

Unfortunately, reassurance does not appear to be the answer. "Reassurance, like dusting, cleans things up for a little while," writes Hallowell (1997: 185), "but then wandering worry reappears." No amount of reassurance is going to talk chronic worriers out of their worry. And despite their endless quest for reassurance, many get angry when reassurance is offered. It is almost as if the worry itself, particularly superstitious worry, is a security blanket. Anyone who dares to snatch it away had better think twice!

If reassurance is not the answer, what is? How can worriers learn to stop worrying without annoying other people in the process? A variety of cognitive, behavioral, and pharmacological treatments have been suggested over the years. Because worry is a type of anxiety, anxiety-reducing medications are often effective. Worriers can also be taught behaviors that give them more control over their worry. They can be taught to stop repetitive negative thoughts before they spiral out of control and to reassure themselves rather than seek reassurance from others. They can be taught to change the way they think about things: to look for the positive rather than immediately assuming the negative and to have faith in their ability to deal with the things they are worried about. Meditation may also help worriers to reduce their level of anxiety and the intrusiveness of their worry.

No amount of medication or behavioral training, however, will keep worriers from occasionally seeking reassurance. But there are strategies that can help them profit from the reassurance they are offered. First, they can be discriminating in selecting the people from whom they seek reassurance. Some people are better able to offer reassurance than others, and some people are more convincing in the reassurance they offer. Thus people who need reassurance should seek it from those who are willing to give it and skilled at doing so (Hallowell, 1997). And second, excessive worriers might concentrate on broadening their social network, so that they will have more people to approach for reassurance. The more people they know to ask for reassurance, the less likely they will be to exhaust the resources of any one person.

7

• • • • • • • •

Deceit and Betrayal

We so highly value our relationships with our families and other people close to us that to lose their trust and respect can be devastating, as Ed discovered:

> I was never able to get away with anything, my parents always found out, and in my senior year of high school I betrayed their trust and confidence once again. My mom found pot in my jacket pocket. She immediately called my dad at work, and we had a "family conference." He threw the bag on the table and told me to start from the beginning about who I got it from, who I smoked it with, how long, etc. Of course, being the immature teenager that I was, I lied about the whole thing. While my mother was crying, he told me to try again—parents *always* know when their kids are lying. Feeling completely ashamed, I told the truth. He threatened to take me to the police station if I did not tell him who I bought the pot from. So I told him and to this day he has that boy's name written down and in the top drawer of his dresser. The next day, he personally took me to the drug and alcohol abuse center to have a drug test. I will never forget how nervous I was. I was eighteen years old when this happened and I sometimes think my parents still worry about what I do in my spare time. It takes a lot of time to gain someone's trust back after you've lost it.

Relationships are critical to our physical and emotional well-being. Ask a group of people whether they would rather spend most of their time alone or with other people and the vast majority will say "with other people." Our need to be accepted by other people is so strong that some researchers consider it a fundamental human motive underlying a significant amount of our behavior.

The relationships that people so eagerly seek and value so highly are also a source of their greatest unhappiness. In fact, relationship problems are one of the primary reasons that people seek professional counseling (Rook, 1998). Although relationships can be threatened by many things, betrayals or breaches of trust figure among the most prominent.

Types of Betrayal

When people enter into relationships, whether with family members, business partners, friends, or marital partners, they bring with them certain beliefs regarding what they can expect from the relationship and from the other person. People expect their spouses to remain faithful to them, their business partners to remain loyal and honest, their friends to be truthful. Teachers expect students to be honest in their academic work and students expect teachers to be fair. As everyone knows, however, these expectations are often violated. The perceived severity of such a betrayal depends on the expectation that has been violated and the nature of the relationship. An adult who fondles a child inappropriately, a husband who cheats on his wife, a student who copies answers from a classmate during an exam—all have violated the trust placed in them and other people's legitimate expectations (Jones and Burdette, 1994).

To determine the specific types of betrayal that people experience, Warren Jones and Marsha Burdette (1994) at the University of Tennessee asked participants to write about betrayals they had suffered and also those of which they had been guilty. The betrayals reported most frequently by both men and women (whether as the victim or the perpetrator) involved extramarital affairs; next in frequency were lies, broken confidences, and two-timing of or by relationship partners. Less common were jilting of relationship partners, failing to support friends and intimate partners, ignoring or avoiding other people, criticism, and gossip. To this list I would add acts of omission—forgetting birthdays or anniversaries, for instance. When such lapses are repeated, they can be just as damaging to a relationship as more blatant forms of betrayal.

Some betrayals can be accidental (Elangovan and Shapiro, 1998). An accidental betrayal sometimes arouses more guilt than an intentional one. If you betray a confidence that you did not know was meant to be kept a secret, you will typically feel a great deal of regret and remorse.

An intentional betrayal can be either premeditated or opportunistic. A betrayal is premeditated if a relationship is established for the sole purpose of later betraying the other person. A case well publicized involved a man named Ronald Shanabarger, who confessed to killing his seven-month-old infant by suffocating him with plastic wrap. His motive was to get revenge on his wife, who before their marriage had failed to cut short a cruise and rush to his side when his father died. Shanabarger had married the woman and fathered her child with the intention of making her suffer by taking the life of the child ("Slay suspect," 1999). The scams of con artists are also premeditated betrayals. These people rarely feel remorse or guilt. Opportunistic betrayal, the most common type, occurs when the betrayer carefully weighs the rewards and costs of violating another's trust, expects the rewards to exceed the costs, and proceeds with the betrayal. Opportunistic betrayals may be premeditated, but relationships are not established for the sole purpose of betraying someone else.

Regardless of their type, all betrayals signal that the relationship between perpetrator and victim is of less value to the betrayer than to the betrayed. It is this perception that makes betrayals so troublesome for the betrayed. Even if they learn to trust their betrayers again, they will have difficulty becoming convinced that the betrayers are actually as committed to the relationship as they once believed.

How Common Is Betrayal?

The frequency of betrayal depends on its type. Lying is probably the most frequent type of betrayal, at least among adults. In fact, lying is so common that most people would probably lie to cover up how much they lie. Most men and women report lying once or twice a day. Over the course of a week they deceive approximately 30 percent of the people with whom they interact (DePaulo et al., 1996). And these are just the lies intended to deceive, not the untruths we tell out of politeness, lies we all tell, such as saying that we're fine when in fact we're not in response to the question "How are you?"

Since people more readily admit little white lies than blatant lies, it is very difficult to gauge how frequent betrayal is. The difficulty is compounded by the fact that many victims are unaware that they have been betrayed. If the question is whether betrayal is more common today than it was thirty or forty years ago, it seems safe to suspect that it probably is. In a survey conducted by *U.S. News and World Report*, 54 percent of the people surveyed felt that people were more deceitful than they had been a decade earlier (Ford, 1996). One reason for an increase in betrayal is that people move more frequently today than they used to. Not expecting to spend the rest of their lives in their new communities, they take little active part in community affairs. When people feel no ongoing connection to the people around them, they are less reluctant to betray them (Carter, 1998). In addition, pressures to succeed seem stronger today than they did a few decades ago. Believing that their honest efforts are unlikely to bring them success, people resort to trickery.

Age-Related Changes in Betrayal

Any attempt to assess the frequency of betrayal should take into account the age of the individuals being surveyed. The most obvious age-related variations are the forms that betrayal takes. The infidelity that Jones and Burdette (1994) found so frequently among adults is less frequent among college students for the simple reason that fewer of them are married; their most common betrayals take the form of two-timing or jilting romantic partners. Lying is the favored betrayal among younger children. Young adults describe fairly recent instances of betrayal; older adults tend to describe betrayals that occurred decades earlier.

Evidence suggests that conceptions of what constitutes betrayal change over time. Most studies of developmental variations in betrayal have focused on lying, in large part because lying is one of the few betrayals that children perpetrate regularly. Children take a broader view of lies than adults do (Lee and Ross, 1997). Children often view any statement that is not factually correct—an exaggeration, say—as a lie. Most adults and children above age eight, however, factor in intentionality when they decide whether something is a lie (Ford, 1996). Thus they consider lies that are intended to help someone as less serious than those that are intended to deceive.

Very young children have little understanding of the consequences of lying. Such understanding comes only with age and training. Before children can lie with the intention to deceive another person, they must have an understanding of themselves as distinct from other people—that other people's beliefs may differ from their own. Until children reach that understanding, about age three, they do not have the capacity to lie (Ford, 1996).

Bella DePaulo and her colleagues (1996) have found some variations in the frequency of lying as a function of age. The adults they interviewed reported lying in approximately one out of every five of their interactions with other people, whereas college students reported lying approximately twice a day. Warren Jones and his colleagues (2001) found that children report lying in a large percentage of their interactions.

The Relationship between
Betrayer and Betrayed

Betrayals occur most frequently between people who are close to one another. Furthermore, DePaulo and her colleagues (1996) found that, although people may tell little white lies to mere acquaintances, they reserve their big lies for their relationship partners.

Men and women as well as victims and perpetrators differ in the specific relationships in which betrayals occur most frequently. In my own research (Kowalski et al., in press), men reported being betrayed and lied to by close friends more often than by romantic partners, acquaintances, or family members. Women also reported being betrayed most frequently by close friends, followed by romantic partners. Women, however, reported being lied to more often by romantic partners than by close friends. One reason for the discrepancy may be that people find it easier to admit being betrayed by a friend than by a romantic partner.

Among betrayers, however, men reported betraying and lying to their romantic partners most often, followed closely by family members. Betrayals of close friends and acquaintances fell far behind. Women said they were more likely to betray a close friend; family members came next. They reported few instances of betraying a romantic partner or acquaintance. As for lying, however, women reported that they were more likely to lie to a family member than to a close friend, romantic partner, or acquaintance. Perhaps betrayal means different things to men and women.

The nature of the relationship between the betrayer and the betrayed has important implications for the effects of the betrayal on one or both of them. To be betrayed by an acquaintance, upsetting and maddening as it is, pales in comparison with betrayal by a close friend or intimate partner. We seldom form an intimate relationship with someone we don't believe we can trust and depend on. When that trust is violated, the betrayal has much greater consequences than a betrayal by a stranger or acquaintance. Indeed, although we can be swindled and cheated by strangers, we should hesitate to say they betrayed us because there was no foundation for the trust we foolishly placed in them.

Reasons People Betray

The reasons people betray someone are probably as varied as the ways they do it. Some people betray because it provides them with an adrenaline rush. Their goal is less a particular outcome than the high of risky behavior. For others, the fear of getting caught in a betrayal is very high but their fear of failure is even higher. Thus they are willing to betray others as a means of promoting their own success. Still others simply believe they can get away with it, so why not?

Because the reasons for betrayal are so many and so various, I have attempted to introduce some order by categorizing them as positive and negative. In general, the positive reasons for betrayal involve the betrayer's concern for the well-being of another person, either the one being betrayed or some third person. The negative reasons for betrayal typically are self-serving. The betrayer violates another person's trust for personal gain.

Before we examine positive and negative motives for betrayal, however, note that the motives people give for their own betrayals often differ from those they attribute to people who betray them. We are typically more forgiving when we are the betrayer than when we have been betrayed. When we have betrayed someone, we typically say that the situation required us to do it, we felt we had no choice; at most we'll admit to being angry or upset—for good reason, of course. When someone has betrayed us, however, we say she's two-faced or he's a back-stabber; she hasn't an honest bone in her body or he can't be trusted as far as you can throw him.

POSITIVE REASONS FOR BETRAYAL

Most people have a hard time thinking of betrayal as positive, but it can be. If you betray a friend in order to reveal that he is sexually abusing a child, for example, the consequences will be positive for the child and for other children who might fall victim to the abuser in the future.

Similarly, people who withhold information in order to protect the feelings of others can be considered to have positive reasons for lying. Kathleen recalled the distress of a friend of hers who was already going bald. Having bought the best hairpiece he could afford—not a good one—he wore it in public one day. "It looked very fake and just awful," Kathleen reported later. "I felt so awkward. He couldn't even look me in the face. Finally after about fifteen minutes of eye-avoiding small talk, he asked me my honest opinion. Of course I lied. I felt so bad, but I thought if this helps his self-esteem, maybe it's okay to lie."

Researchers have found that approximately 25 percent of the lies people tell are told for the benefit of someone else. They are told to avoid embarrassment and awkwardness or to avoid hurting someone's feelings ("Honesty," 1999). A broken promise is surely a betrayal, yet it, too, can be motivated by concern for another person, as we see in Michael's account: "In my sophomore year of high school, I was dating a girl who had a real problem. She was anorexic and she didn't realize it. At first, I denied it too. She ended up in the hospital, weighing in at 48 pounds with a resting heart rate under 30. She was about to die, it was so bad. Before she was admitted to the hospital, it got to a point where I couldn't face it anymore. I'd promised her I would never tell anybody about her problem, but I had to. I went against my promise for her own good."

Some people refer to lies that are in the best interests of others as kind lies (Kornet, 1997). We are telling a kind lie when we tell an actor we liked his performance better than we did or our far-sighted grandmother that we really love the ill-fitting sweater she made for us. Such lies not only bolster the self-esteem of the targets but act as social lubricants (Kornet, 1997). DePaulo and her colleagues (1996) have found that women are more likely than men to tell kind lies, confirming the image of women as more concerned with relationships than men and as more protective of other people's feelings.

Lies and betrayals may also be perpetrated to protect the image of a third person. Sarah told me of discovering that a close family friend who she thought had died of cancer had in fact died of AIDS. In an attempt to understand why her mother had lied to her, she said, "I think she thought I might not understand and didn't want me to view him differently."

Finally, betrayals, particularly lies, may be perpetrated to avoid conflict (Metts, 1999; Peterson, 1996). If you know that your partner would be upset to know you had lunch with an attractive co-worker, you may lie and say you had lunch with your brother instead. If your partner believes you, a conflict has been avoided.

Sometimes, though, even lies told with the best of intentions can backfire. Kathleen, who lied to her friend about how his hair-piece looked, said, "Eventually I realized that the truth would have been better. Maybe if I'd told him it looked bad, he would have taken it off and spared himself embarrassment. He continued to wear a piece for about two years and then finally gave it up and got a crew cut."

Of course, whether the reason for a betrayal is positive or negative depends on whether one is the betrayer or the betrayed. In an attempt to justify their actions, some betrayers give positive reasons for their behavior, even though it is highly unlikely that the person who has been betrayed takes the same view of it. One man who was having an affair with a woman at work said he was doing his wife a favor "by not imposing his sexual requirements upon her" ("Rule of honesty," 1999).

NEGATIVE REASONS FOR BETRAYAL

Anyone who regularly betrays other people's trust is probably not engaging in betrayal for positive reasons. One of the most common reasons is that betrayal looks like an easy way out of some personal difficulty. Some students see copying from someone else's paper as much easier than actually studying for a test. Embezzlers view appropriating money as easier than earning it. Such betrayals reflect basic selfishness; the betrayer gives little thought to the consequences for others.

Sometimes, however, the reason for betrayal may simply reflect what experience has taught us to expect from other people. In *Love and Betrayal* John Amodeo discusses what he refers to as the "childhood legacy of betrayal." People who were betrayed as children and consequently felt they were not valued often have trouble in their adult relationships. Having learned to expect rejection, they may behave in ways that lead them to be rejected. By being withdrawn or overly aggressive, for example, they turn their fear of rejection into a self-fulfilling prophecy. Or, feeling certain that others will betray them, they may decide to beat them to the punch and become the betrayers themselves.

People who learn to expect betrayal usually have learned it in childhood from their parents. How many children have been punished for lying, for example, only to witness their parents lying? Thus betrayal, even betrayal involving little white lies, may develop simply as a result of learning and imitating.

A third cause of betrayal is unrealistic expectations on the part of either the betrayer or the betrayed. Betrayers often have unrealistic expectations as to just how well relationships are supposed to function. All relationships have their ups and downs. People who can ride out the downs are not likely to be as frustrated by them as people who expect relationships always to flow smoothly. Such unrealistic expectations may lead people to betray the ones who have disillusioned them.

Unrealistic expectations may also set one up to be betrayed. A person who expects too much from a relationship may repeatedly make excessive demands. Such people want more than most of us have to give. In response to the repeated pressure and failure to please, their partners may lie about why they have not lived up to the expectations or may seek more fulfilling relationships elsewhere.

Fourth, betrayal may follow from competing obligations or desires (Baxter et al., 1997). I would venture to guess that virtually everyone has canceled at least one date or appointment because a more appealing alternative presented itself. In such a situation, you generally tell a little white lie to explain why you can't keep the original date. Similar competing desires arise when feelings of obligation to spend time with one's spouse compete with one's desire to spend time with friends (Baxter et al., 1997). Occasionally you may lie about your whereabouts in order to spend time with friends.

Finally, the most negative reason for betrayal is a desire to hurt the victim, perhaps but not necessarily to get revenge for a betrayal by the victim. Lies that are told or secrets that are disclosed for

How Likely Are You to Betray?

People obviously differ in their readiness to betray others. Although many people may be unwilling to admit that they would betray anyone, they may be tripped up by measures developed to determine how likely they are to do so. One such measure, the Interpersonal Betrayal Scale, consists of fifteen items covering a range of types of betrayal (see p. 155).

To complete the scale, simply rate how often you have performed the behavior described in each statement, using the 5-point scale provided. Then add up the points you have assigned to the items. Scores range from 15 to 75 points; the average score for college students is approximately 36. For adults not in college, the average for both men and women is about 35. Among older adults, the average score is 28 (Jones and Burdette, 1994).

Having administered the scale to hundreds of people, Warren Jones and Marsha Burdette determined that certain types of people are indeed more likely to betray than others. As the average scores indicate, younger people are more likely to betray than older people. In addition, white respondents show a stronger tendency to betray than minority respondents. People whose jobs bring them into frequent contact with other people, such as attorneys, are more likely to betray than people who work in more solitary occupations, such as carpentry. People who are not religious also had higher betrayal scores than the devout. When people who completed the scale were asked to describe themselves, those who scored high in a tendency to betray used such adjectives as "jealous," "vengeful," "morose," and "pompous."

the sole purpose of hurting another person fall into this category. Betrayals of this sort do indeed hurt the victim, but they also generally have negative repercussions for the betrayer. It is one thing to be perceived as a betrayer; it is another to be viewed as a malicious one.

Table 7.1. Interpersonal Betrayal Scale

Read each item and respond to it using the scale below:

       1 = I have never done this

       2 = I have done this once

       3 = I have done this a few times

       4 = I have done this several times

       5 = I have done this many times

_____ 1. Snubbing a friend when with a group you want to impress.

_____ 2. Breaking a promise without a good reason.

_____ 3. Agreeing with people you really disagree with so that they will accept you.

_____ 4. Pretending to like someone you detest.

_____ 5. Gossiping about a friend behind his/her back.

_____ 6. Making a promise to a friend with no intention of keeping it.

_____ 7. Failing to stand up for what you believe in because you want to be accepted by the "in crowd."

_____ 8. Complaining to others about your friends or family members.

_____ 9. Telling others information given to you in confidence.

_____ 10. Lying to a friend.

_____ 11. Making a promise to a family member with no intention of keeping it.

_____ 12. Failing to stand up for a friend when criticized or belittled by others.

_____ 13. Taking family members for granted.

_____ 14. Lying to parents/spouse about activities.

_____ 15. Wishing that something bad would happen to someone you dislike.

Source: W. H. Jones and M. P. Burdette, "Betrayal in Relationships," in W. L. Weber and J. H. Harvey, eds., *Perspectives on Close Relationships,* 251. Copyright © 1994 by Allyn and Bacon. Reprinted by permission.

Victims' and Perpetrators' Perceptions of Betrayal

Victims and perpetrators usually have very different perceptions of betrayal. Betrayers may not even consider their actions to be betrayals. A man who gets home an hour later than he was expected, for example, is unlikely to feel that he has betrayed his wife, but she may feel so betrayed that she may wonder if she will ever be able to trust him again.

More generally, Warren Jones and his colleagues (2001) found that perpetrators view betrayal as much less serious than victims do and see fewer negative consequences. Furthermore, betrayers tend to attribute their transgressions to something external to themselves—peer pressure, say, or their partner's behavior, or a situation over which they had no control. Victims attribute betrayers' indiscretions to the character of the betrayers—their impulsiveness, their insensitivity, their stupidity, their lack of commitment.

Perpetrators are more likely than victims to blame themselves. Feelings of guilt may explain why betrayers who decide to reveal their betrayal to the victim often fail to do so face to face. They may confess in a letter or even in a phone call. Some simply allow their victims to hear about the betrayal from other people.

In our own investigations (Kowalski et al., in press), we have found fairly consistent differences in the perceptions of betrayal by victims and perpetrators. Betrayers consider betrayal less troublesome and less damaging to the relationship than victims do. Yet we found no differences in victims' and perpetrators' ratings of the hurt suffered by victims. It appears, then, that betrayers are well aware of the damage their behavior inflicts on their victims—it just doesn't trouble them much.

Consequences of Lying and Betrayal

The type of betrayal and the nature of the relationship between the victim and the betrayer determine how serious the consequences are. Little white lies told for the benefit of another person typically have fewer negative consequences than blatant lies that are intended to deceive. Over time, however, even small betrayals can gradually chip away at one's trust, so that ultimately the consequences may be as serious as those of more extreme betrayals. Suppose you enjoy volunteer work at the local crisis center but your partner resents the time you spend on it. You feel that the work is valuable and that your partner is being petty to object, so you make up a series of excuses to account for your whereabouts—too many to be believable. Even if you have been absolutely faithful, your "little" lies may so erode your partner's trust that your relationship will suffer. Meanwhile, you have done nothing to solve the real problem—your partner's unreasonable objections to your doing worthwhile work that you enjoy.

When you think of the consequences of betrayal, you generally think of the consequences for the victim. The pain, heartache, disillusionment, anger, and mistrust seem to belong exclusively to the victim. There are consequences, however, often very serious ones, for the betrayer as well.

DAMAGE TO THE RELATIONSHIP

All betrayals have consequences. Although some people report that a betrayal served to strengthen their relationship, it is far more common for betrayal to damage a relationship; some never recover. Reestablishing trust, if it is possible at all, can take years. The uncertainty that follows violations of trust is often too much for some people. They are constantly on the watch for clues to betrayal. Obviously the damage to the relationship will depend on its strength before the betrayal, the nature of the betrayal, and the number of people who know about it. One sexual betrayal outweighs a dozen criticisms. Betrayals that are known only to the betrayer and the betrayed tend to have fewer negative effects than betrayals of which other people are aware. When other people know, public humiliation is heaped on private pain (Metts, 1998). In addition, perceptions of the degree of damage to the relationship depend on whether you are the victim or the betrayer. Jones and Burdette (1994) have found that over 90 percent of victims report that their relationship with the betrayer was made worse by the betrayal. Only about 40 percent of betrayers, however, reported that the relationship had deteriorated; another 40 percent said it had remained unchanged and 20 percent said it had improved.

Satisfaction with a relationship declines abruptly when one partner deceives the other. Candida Peterson (1996) found that people who admitted lying to their relationship partner or who acknowledged that their partner lied to them reported less satisfaction in their relationships than people in relationships that were not strained by deception. Of course, dissatisfaction with a relationship can also precipitate betrayal in the first place. Proof of the relationship damage that can follow from betrayal is poignantly seen in Tom's experience:

> My sophomore year of high school, I was expressing to my father how concerned I was about making it to college. I came from a poor family and realized that it would take a lot of money as well as hard work and determination to make it into a good school by earning various grants and scholarships. My dad made me a promise that cold, fall morning in our dirt driveway in rural southern California. I remember it like it just happened. He looked at me and said, "Son, don't worry about all that. You've worked too hard for too long. You deserve the best, and between your grandfather and me, we're going to make sure you get into college." This single statement motivated me to try harder than ever. By the end of my junior year in high school, I was promoted to group commander of my Air Force Junior ROTC, with the responsibility of overseeing the functioning of over 200 cadets below me, . . . I was turning out to be an amazing leader, well respected by my peers and beginning to turn the heads of area military recruiters as well as school faculty and college area representatives from all over the United States, military academies included. . . . I had climbed through the ranks so fast that I was

promoted to cadet colonel (the highest rank available) by the end of the first semester of my senior year. My tenure as group commander ended with the end of the fall semester and I had a whole semester to . . . work on narrowing my college choices down. I made my final selection for an Army four-year scholarship to the school of my choice and was guaranteed three years. The only thing I needed was to go to the local Air Force base and take another test. The Army gave me one week to do this. My stepmother, the only transportation I was allowed to have, continuously forgot about appointment after appointment, causing time to expire and my application to be totally withdrawn from competition. I got nothing. All of my time and energy was wasted. After this defeat I was thankful not to have put all my eggs in one basket. I was accepted to Clemson and things were going good. I had it all taken care of until the university asked me to verify some tax information of my father's for financial aid purposes. My father never returned my calls, time expired. I found myself working at K-Mart, a crushing defeat. He had broken his promise, he had lied, he had betrayed me. It only made it worse to find out that my father's pride had kept him from telling me that congressional nominations to the Air Force Academy and West Point had come in the mail as well as acceptance letters from Virginia Military Academy and the Citadel. It has taken me a long time to get over this. I am not sure if I am over it yet.

Betrayal can not only have detrimental consequences for the relationship between the betrayer and the betrayed; it can also damage later relationships with other people. A victim of marital infidelity, for example, may feel that she will never again be able to trust anyone. A student whose best friend had become involved with her boyfriend said, "I haven't spoken to either since. It really hurt me and it made it even harder to trust someone."

In addition to finding it difficult to trust other people, victims may feel somehow responsible for the betrayal and assume that they are unlovable. Their self-esteem may plummet. After Elizabeth cheated on her boyfriend, she reported, "He got very depressed, and he thought something was wrong with him." Burdened by such feelings, victims may hesitate to pursue other relationships for fear that once again they will be rejected.

This is a particular danger for people who are sensitive to rejection anyway. If they do manage to establish a relationship, they may be so fearful of rejection that they behave in ways that lead their partner to reject them (Downey et al., 1998). A man whose wife badgers him to give a minute account of his whereabouts during his time away from home or a woman whose husband, with no evidence, repeatedly accuses her of having an affair is quite likely to find the relationship too dissatisfying to sustain.

The length of time required to repair a relationship that has been damaged varies with the seriousness of the betrayal. Sometimes, even though the relationship remains intact, complete trust is never restored, as Laura discovered:

> I was dating a guy at the time and we were not really serious, but we had kind of nonverbally narrowed down to just dating each other. Not wanting to get serious at the time, but not wanting to quit seeing this guy, I lied when I told him I went out with a couple of girlfriends after work when, in actuality, I went out with a guy I worked with. The guy I was dating seemed suspicious but did not question me. But, feeling guilty two years later and wanting to make a clean start, I confessed. It had a very negative effect on us. We are still together today but it has taken eight years to really be able to talk and for him to trust me. Even today, it still affects what we do! If I am late getting home, et cetera . . . he wonders where I have been but never asks.

At the extreme, the consequences of betrayal may be fatal, particularly for the perpetrator. Many people have killed a spouse or partner who has been cheating or is simply suspected of cheating.

Lying, too, can have deadly consequences. People who lie to their sex partners about their HIV status, for example, are jeopardizing their partners' lives. What begins as a lie may end in death.

EMOTIONAL DAMAGE

Both the betrayer and the betrayed experience a wide variety of emotional reactions to the betrayal, most of them negative. One of the most common emotions reported by betrayers is guilt, as reflected in Charlie's account:

> My friends and I took my parents' car out for a ride. While driving, we decided to take the car on a wooded path that was not designed for cars. In the process, both front doors were dented by trees. I lied to my parents, saying that the dents had been put into the car while we were in a department store. Afterward I felt badly because I had never done anything to gain my parents' distrust. Four years later, I told my mother, somewhat out of a childhood memory that now seemed funny but also to get it off my chest.

Many betrayers also report feeling angry. Although the anger may stem from having been found out, it may also be an attempt to justify the betrayal. Betrayers who direct anger toward their victims displace blame from themselves to the ones they have betrayed.

Betrayers may also feel relief when the betrayal has become known. It takes a lot of physical and emotional energy to keep a secret or to try to cover up a lie. Once the betrayal becomes known or the falsehood is revealed, a sense of relief follows, even if other negative consequences can be expected.

To deal with the negative emotions that may accompany their betrayals, betrayers can generate an amazing array of justifications for their actions. For example, Dion Lee, a basketball player involved in a point-shaving scandal, initially justified his actions by saying that the team was already losing, so he wasn't really causing the team to lose. By contrast, a guest on the Oprah Winfrey show justified her regular cheating of the Internal Revenue Service by claiming, "It's okay if no one really gets hurt." Still others justify their actions by saying, "Everyone else is doing it, so why shouldn't I?"

Emotional reactions are typically much more numerous and more negative for the person who has been betrayed. Victims may feel hurt, angry, depressed, anxious, afraid, and ashamed. They may feel something must be wrong with them, or why would someone betray them or lie to them? "What's wrong with me?" they wonder. "What could I have done differently?" A young woman who had been fondled as a child by a family friend said, "I was too afraid to tell anyone for years, although I can't remember him telling me not to tell. I just know how worthless and dirty I felt for a very long time."

Rage and anger are common. Judy reported, "Some friends and I were standing around talking. One of them left so I told the rest of my friends the secret that she had told me the night before, and asked me not to tell anyone. When I was in the middle of sharing her secret with the rest of the group, she came back and I didn't know. She was mad for a long time." As long as it does not get out of hand, anger may actually be adaptive for the person who has been betrayed. As long as victims are angry at the betrayer, it is more difficult for them to blame themselves for the betrayal.

To deal with the emotional fallout of betrayal, some victims seek revenge. Such instances, however, account for less than one-fourth of cases (Jones et al., 2001). Other victims—not many—decide to forgive the betrayer. Forgiveness, of course, depends on the betrayal (certainly a little white lie is more easily forgiven than infidelity) and on an array of other factors: the betrayer's remorse, the time that passes between the betrayal and an apology, the frequency of betrayal, the benefit of the betrayal to the betrayer, and the justifications offered for it. Betrayers who show little or no remorse, who have betrayed more than once, who delay in apologizing or never apologize, who appear to benefit from the betrayal, and who offer ludicrous justifications or excuses or none at all are unlikely to be forgiven.

Any betrayal implies that the betrayer places little value on the relationship. That's what makes forgiveness so difficult. It's not just that our trust has been violated; it's that the relationship that means so much to us obviously means far less to the betrayer. Even if the betrayer never betrays us again, how can we ever be convinced that the one who has betrayed us now values our relationship as we do? Even if we do forgive, forgiveness does not necessarily imply true reconciliation.

If victims do not seek revenge and cannot bring themselves to forgive the betrayer, they may fall into quiet resignation. Although they may choose not to confront the betrayer, they remain ever vigilant for signs of betrayal. Such people are typically those who feel that they somehow brought on the betrayal or that they are unworthy of unconditional love and therefore must expect to be betrayed. The betrayal may deal such a blow to their self-esteem that they fall into depression.

What Can We Do about Betrayal?

Although it is unrealistic to expect to eliminate betrayals from our lives, there are some steps we can take to minimize their frequency and lessen the toll they take. If we can learn to communicate effectively, to maintain realistic expectations, and to balance our own interests against the interests of our partner, we will go a long way toward buffering our relationships against the catastrophes that betrayal can inflict.

COMMUNICATION

Perhaps the best way to prevent betrayal is through communication. Friends and partners in relationship often fail to communicate their minor hurts and disappointments, perhaps out of fear of conflict, until they have developed into major dissatisfactions. At that point, any confrontation is likely to be met with defensiveness, disillusionment, and perhaps betrayal. As Amodeo (1994) has said, "Learning to contact feelings and concerns at an earlier moment, then exploring these issues together, may avert a blind drift toward conflict and misunderstanding" (160).

Even after a betrayal, communication can help to bring a relationship back on track or at least prevent further damage to it. When we catch our partner in a lie, for instance, it will do our relationship no good to stifle our anger or refuse to discuss it. The expression of our anger is healthy as long as it is done in a way that avoids insults and shame (Amodeo, 1994).

Part of learning to communicate is learning the skills necessary for constructive conflict resolution (Peterson, 1996). Therapists or counselors can be very useful in helping us develop such skills.

MAINTAINING REALISTIC EXPECTATIONS

Learning to moderate our expectations may decrease the likelihood that we will either betray or be betrayed. No person can satisfy all your needs. To expect that much of another person is to expect too much. The pressure to be all things to you may lead your partner to withdraw from you, lie to you, or seek a less stressful relationship elsewhere.

If your expectations are realistic, you will at least occasionally give the other person the benefit of the doubt. When we are racked by insecurities or when our friends and relationship partners have given us reason in the past to doubt their trustworthiness, trusting them is very difficult. When you do show your trust, however, your friend or partner may at least think twice about betraying it.

It is natural for relationships to change with time. The euphoria of the early days and months of a relationship cannot be sustained forever. Particularly when you spend increasing amounts of time together, it is unrealistic to expect either of you to be on your best behavior at all times. The effort that people put into their friendships and relationships early on will certainly be reduced as familiarity and competing demands enter the picture. These changes do not have to signal problems in the relationship or lead to situations in which betrayal becomes likely.

Finally, maintaining realistic expectations may prevent you from seeing betrayal where there is none. We begin to feel rejected when it seems to us that the person we care about no longer cares so much about us. But the problem may lie in our unrealistic expectations. Your friend can't spend every weekend with you, after all; it's unrealistic to expect her to. And your father's reluctance to rent a truck and drive three hundred miles to bring you the old sofa you want for your apartment doesn't mean he doesn't love you.

BALANCING YOUR INTERESTS AGAINST THE OTHER PERSON'S INTERESTS

Betrayals, like so many other troublesome behaviors, often occur when people put their own interests above those of other people. If we took more account of other people's perspectives, betrayals would probably be much less common than they are. Knowing the damage that could result from a betrayal, we would think twice before lying to our romantic partner or revealing a confidence we had promised not to reveal. Betrayals would still happen, but we could hope that most of them would be of the kind intended for the benefit of other people. Our relationships are too important to us to be jeopardized by the cruelty we inflict by selfish betrayal.

● ● ● ● ● ● ● ●
Epilogue

As a part of the . . . Community,
I will pledge to be a part of the solution.
I will eliminate taunting from my own behavior.
I will encourage others to do the same.
I will do my part to make . . . a safe place by being more
   sensitive to others.
I will set the example of a caring individual.
I will eliminate profanity towards others from my language.
I will not let my words or actions hurt others.
. . . and if others won't become part of the solution, I WILL.
                  —Pledge written by students at Hillsboro High School,
                                    Nashville, Tennessee, 1999

After making a pit stop, a colleague of mine walked by my office
the other day commenting on how annoying it is to find the toilet
unflushed. From there he went on to talk about other things people do that he finds annoying, among them littering and smoking.
His observations highlighted to me the pervasiveness of annoying
behaviors; they are our constant companions.

As you read this book, you may have been struck by the considerable overlap in the behaviors I have been discussing. To talk
about one annoying behavior often necessitates talking about an-

other. Complaining about your significant other to a close friend, for example, may be interpreted as a betrayal. Bullies often intimidate other people to convey their self-perceived superiority. Narcissists, despite their apparent self-satisfaction, often suffer from problems with dependency and feelings of inadequacy. Dependent people are characterized by neediness and excessive reliance on others. Chronic worriers often complain to other people about their concerns.

Because of the considerable overlap in the behaviors that are discussed in this book, it should not be surprising that they share a number of features, which I will examine in the pages that follow. In addition, by offering suggestions for ways in which we can learn to be kinder and more considerate of others in our daily interactions and by presenting ways we can learn to respond to others' obnoxiousness, I would like to develop the theme suggested by the pledge that began this epilogue. that we learn to be part of the solution rather than the problem.

The Inevitability of Obnoxiousness

Recently I was reading a book edited by Jeremiah Abrams and Connie Zweig titled *Meeting the Shadow: The Hidden Power of the Dark Side of Human Nature* (1991). In the preface the editors allude to the Jekyll and Hyde personalities in every individual. For all the kindness and politeness we display, we are also at times harsh, mean, and rude. Such negative behaviors are what Zweig and Abrams refer to as the "personal shadow." As they put it, "Negative emotions and behaviors—rage, jealousy, shame, lying, resentment, lust, greed, suicidal and murderous tendencies—lie concealed just below the surface, masked by our more proper selves" (xvi). Often little provocation is required, unfortunately, for any one of these behaviors to raise its ugly head above the surface. They assault us every day. We cannot avoid them.

The Frequency of Obnoxious Behaviors

Not only are obnoxious behaviors inevitable, they are frequent and apparently becoming more so (Kowalski, 1997). People seem to be increasingly dissatisfied and ever readier to complain. Since the 1960s people seem to have become less concerned about the feelings of others. Thus they are less hesitant than earlier to engage in malicious teasing or to behave in ways that make others feel inferior. If surveys are any indication, instances of betrayal and lying are also on the rise.

Part of this increase in the frequency of annoying behaviors may be our own fault. Perhaps we have become tolerant and forgiving of behaviors that once were not tolerated. People may swear more frequently now (at least publicly) than in years past because we have become tolerant of such incivility. More people than ever before may be narcissistic, yet these are the very people that we appoint as our national leaders. We seem so concerned about the impressions that other people form of us that we rarely inform them when we are fed up with their complaining, teasing, or other annoying behaviors.

If the frequency of these annoying behaviors has indeed increased, what can we expect in the future? Will we just continue to hurt other people's feelings? Will incivility in the workplace and at home simply continue to increase? My hunch is that there will be a point at which we become so fed up with rudeness, incivility, and nastiness that we'll begin to move in the other direction. Although we may still see increases in some of the behaviors, I venture to predict that many of them have reached their peak as far as frequency is concerned. Remember that people may have specific goals in mind when they engage in annoying behaviors: they want to bolster their self-esteem or control someone else. Such behavior can backfire, however, thwarting an attempt to achieve the outcome it was designed to attain. Thus a point is reached at which we no longer tolerate it.

Of course, throughout history people have complained, teased, betrayed, and been uncivil. So, although the frequency of these behaviors may have increased, they are nothing new. We can hope that their frequency will decline, but it would be unrealistic to expect to eliminate them.

Broadening the Scope

All the behaviors I have been examining have been considered primarily as interpersonal problems—irritating or hostile actions directed by one person against another. Many such behaviors, however, can be perpetrated by societies or entire countries. Racial prejudice is pervasive. Societies go to war because of their narcissistic conviction of the superiority of their own race or religion or way of life. Germans try to wipe out Jews and gypsies; Bosnians attempt to annihilate Serbs, and Serbs set out to "cleanse" their society of Muslims. Fundamentalist Muslims, for their part, launch a war of terror against "infidels." As Jeremiah Abrams and Connie Zweig (1991) noted, "Today we are confronted with the dark side of human nature each time we open a newspaper or watch the evening news. . . . The world has become a stage for the collective shadow. The collective shadow . . . is staring back at us virtually everywhere" (xx).

All obnoxious behaviors, whether at the interpersonal or societal level and whatever their intention, frequently create more problems than they were expected to solve. If, in an effort to improve your relationship with your husband, you complain time after time that when he tells you he won't be home for dinner, he simply must stop expecting to find dinner waiting for him when he arrives at 9 P.M., your complaining may become more annoying than the annoying behavior you were attempting to change by complaining. Victims of repeated bullying have retaliated with guns. No country has ever sent its young men and women to war without being sure it was engaging in a righteous struggle against evil enemies.

Emotional Contagion

The central problem with all the behaviors examined here is that they produce psychological and even physical distress in the victim. Research has shown that anxiety, depression, and even harmful physical changes can stem from a single insulting or demeaning social interaction (Farina, Wheeler, and Mehta, 1991). Imagine, then, the long-term effects of repeated exposure to such behaviors.

One way in which annoying social interactions produce their harmful effects is through emotional contagion, or the passing of an emotion from one person to another. The emotion passed by good-natured teasing will generally be positive; the emotions transmitted by bullying will be negative. All annoying behaviors elicit negative emotions; that's why we call them annoying. Unfortunately, these negative emotional states may then be passed on to others, who pass them on to still others, and so on. Thus a single person's annoying behavior can produce a ripple of unhappiness and frustration that spreads like the ripples produced by a stone thrown into a pond.

Perceived Meaning of the Behaviors

People will withstand a great deal of unpleasantness as long as they can find positive meaning in the events or actions that produce it (Baumeister, 1991). The meaning assigned to a behavior by a victim, however, will differ from the meaning assigned by a perpetrator. Perpetrators always take a more benign view of their behavior than their victims do.

Even among victims and among perpetrators, the meaning of a behavior may vary. In our own research (Kowalski et al., in press), women indicated that they were more likely to betray and complain to a close friend than to a romantic partner or acquaintance, whereas men reported a higher likelihood of betraying and complaining to a romantic partner than to a close friend or acquaintance. On the other hand, men were more likely to seek reassurance from a close friend whereas women reported being more likely to seek reassurance from a romantic partner. Clearly men and women were not assigning the same meaning to the behaviors.

Thus the unpleasantness of a behavior and the meaning assigned to it depend on who is doing the evaluating. Many behaviors we call annoying, among them arrogance and dependency, are not traits or stable characteristics but rather inferences or conclusions that we draw about another person (Hallmark and Curtis, 1994). Some people are simply more likely than others to perceive other people's behavior as annoying. A person who is highly sensitive to rejection is predisposed to see signs of rejection in other people's behavior. No matter how well intentioned another person's teasing may be, the rejection-sensitive person will see it as malicious. People high in self-esteem seem to have a buffer that protects them against feelings of rejection. Feeling good about themselves, they are quite prepared to see good in others.

One's readiness to attach negative meaning to another person's behavior also varies with the nature of the relationship between them. Research has shown that couples who are dissatisfied with their relationships are far more likely than satisfied couples to attribute their partner's behavior to ill will.

In addition, the meaning one attaches to a behavior depends on one's culture. What is considered normal in one culture may be considered abnormal in another; what is considered annoying in one culture may be considered normal or even pleasurable in another. Some of the cultural differences we observe depend on whether the culture is individualistic or collectivist. People in an individualistic culture, such as the United States, are typically more concerned with themselves than with others. They value their individuality and independence and define themselves as individuals first and as part of a collective—their workplace, their social group, their school, their state—second. People in a collectivist society, such as Japan, put the collective before the individual. The values and expectations of the group are given far more weight than any individual strivings. For this reason, annoying behaviors such as teasing are less likely to be perpetrated for personal gain in a collectivist culture, at least not without some serious consequences. To put down a member of the collective is to risk being ostracized, unless, of course, teasing is being used to make someone conform to the collective. Teasing in an individualistic culture, while not necessarily making one the most popular person, can raise one's status.

Because many variables can influence the meaning attached to behaviors, one way to conceptualize them is to place each on a continuum from normal to unpleasant. Since everyone has a degree of narcissism, motivated by a desire to maintain a favorable view of the self, and since everyone complains, at least occasionally, neither narcissism nor complaining can automatically be assigned to the unpleasant end of the continuum. It is only when complaining becomes too frequent or narcissism is displayed in an inappropriate context that it becomes unpleasant. Viewing behaviors on a continuum, then, allows for individual and cultural differences in the meanings people attach to them.

Failures of Self-Control

If we really tried, probably all of us could behave more appropriately and respectfully toward others. If we put forth just a little extra effort, we could withhold complaints that no one really wants to hear or we could stop ourselves from teasing someone who is sensitive to signs of rejection. With a little more attention and effort, we could resist acting in arrogant ways that make others feel bad, and we could avoid telling lies that hurt others. But even if we did exercise such self-control, for how long could we do so? And if we refrain from complaining today, does our forbearance make it easier to stop ourselves from doing something else annoying tomorrow?

The social psychologists Mark Muraven and Roy Baumeister (2000) have raised just such questions. In their strength model of self-regulation or self-control, they suggest that self-control operates much like a muscle: once we have used it, we have temporarily depleted its resources; it needs time to recover before it will function well again. If complaining is a dominant response and we stop ourselves from complaining, we'll find it more difficult to stop ourselves from doing something else annoying shortly thereafter. But people differ in their initial levels of self-control. People who start with higher levels of self-control will have less difficulty exercising self-control again than people who start with low levels of self-control.

Repeated attempts to control ourselves affect not only our ability to refrain from doing annoying things but also the degree of annoyingness other people find in our behavior. When you are annoyed by my behavior, your first reaction may be to give me the benefit of the doubt. Maybe I was complaining because I was truly having a bad day. If I go on and on complaining, however, you will find it harder and harder to control your annoyance. As time goes on, you find your resources for self-control exhausted.

The difficulty of self-regulation makes it quite understandable that "the majority of contemporary social and personal problems afflicting Western society contained some element of self-regulation failure" (Dale and Baumeister, 1999: 139–40). Indeed, it is primarily because of the difficulty of controlling ourselves that annoying behaviors are so common. If we could exercise self-control more consistently, the frequency of our own and other people's annoying behaviors would surely decrease.

Consequences of Annoying Behaviors

All annoying behaviors have negative consequences. Two that we have seen repeatedly are relationship difficulties and aggression.

Annoying behaviors can create more stress than a relationship can stand. Because we are sick of listening to incessant complaints or of being hurt by inconsiderate narcissism, we may withdraw from the person who is making us feel bad. Should the offensive behavior not stop, we may choose to end the relationship. Perhaps the best predictor of the dissolution of a relationship is what is called relational devaluation: behaviors that are perceived to indicate that one's partner places little value on the relationship hurt more than behaviors for which more positive motives may be found (Leary and Springer, 2001). People will end a relationship that offers only belittlement and disrespect rather than continue to endure it.

The aggression that occurs in response to other people's obnoxious behaviors often seems out of proportion to the behavior that prompted it, but the rage that such behaviors can provoke is very real. Many instances of domestic violence and homicide stem from instances of betrayal. When other drivers unintentionally cut us off on the road, we feel just as angry as if they had done it deliberately. It is certainly not uncommon for people to perceive more malice than was ever intended. If malice was indeed behind the behavior that enraged us, aggression is more understandable but still is seldom appropriate. There are better ways of responding to behaviors we dislike.

Why Tolerate It?

You may wonder why people continue to put up with behaviors that hurt and anger them. Any behavior that occurs infrequently can generally be tolerated. But what about constant exposure to an array of obnoxious behaviors, with no hope in sight that they will ever end? In such situations, some people do simply end the relationship and try to find a more satisfying relationship elsewhere. But others continue to put up with endless hurts and even physical abuse. Why?

The answer seems to lie in our need to be included. Roy Baumeister and Mark Leary (1995) have suggested that the need to belong is a fundamental motive that underlies a great deal of human behavior. According to their theory of belongingness, people who do not feel included by others experience such a host of negative effects that they will go to great lengths to maintain relationships, even if those relationships are dissatisfying. They may get no social support from those relationships and they may experience a lot of pain as they struggle to maintain them, but they still have the satisfaction of being connected to some person or group. How many times have you chosen to spend time with people you really don't like just so you won't have to be by yourself? At such times your need to belong overrides the negative feelings those people arouse. The same logic helps to explain why some women remain in abusive relationships. Although other factors can enter into the situation (fear of being killed if they try to leave, inability to provide for their children), some women may stay with an abuser because any relationship, however painful, seems better than being alone.

The irony of the belongingness theory is that being rejected or excluded may trigger annoying behaviors in the victim. People who have been rejected may sink into dependency or turn to aggression. The rejection one suffers may impair one's control over selfish, antisocial impulses (Twenge, 2000).

What to Do

The way we handle other people's annoying behavior depends on why we think they are engaging in it. Some people are seemingly unaware that they are being annoying. Once the irritation produced by their behavior is pointed out to them, they typically appear quite willing to try to do better. Other people know they are annoying but have no idea how to stop. People who seek reassurance to control their anxiety, for example, may be unable to stop seeking reassurance. As Hallowell (1997) has said, "Most worriers know they worry too much. . . . They know it is annoying to others. . . . But they cannot stop" (184). Still others use their annoying behaviors to manipulate others. Betrayal and lying are used almost exclusively for that purpose. Finally, people may behave in annoying ways to gain attention. Many people who go in for good-natured teasing are doing so to draw attention to themselves. The table below shows the reasons for the various behaviors discussed here. Certainly if we perceive that someone is being annoying for personal gain or to manipulate us, we will react to the behavior very differently than we would if we found the person simply couldn't stop it.

Once we understand why the person is doing something that annoys us, we can more easily decide what course of action we want to take. Although the choice of action will depend on the behavior, we would do well to remember that, although we can't always change other people, we can change the impact their behavior has on us. You have probably heard it said that other people

Table Epi.1. Reasons for Annoying Behaviors

Behavior	Can't stop	Don't realize doing it	Manipulation	Attention-seeking
Teasing			✓	✓
Complaining	✓	✓	✓	✓
Narcissism		✓	✓	✓
Worry	✓	✓	✓	✓
Impropriety				✓
Betrayal			✓	

don't make one angry, rather one allows other people to make one angry. Obnoxiousness is in the eye of the beholder. What annoys one person is good-natured fun to someone else. Thus it is possible that other people really don't mean to be annoying but, for one reason or another, their behavior hits a nerve with us. In such cases, the burden is on us. We must find a way to deal with behaviors that we find annoying so that they no longer get on our nerves.

One thing we can do is try to get other people to see themselves as we see them. If we can do that, the frequency with which they perpetrate annoying behaviors is likely to decrease. Most people who are made aware of their own behavior report feeling uncomfortable when they focus on themselves; they are not very happy with what they see. Not all people react this way, however. Narcissists actually seek out situations that allow them to view themselves much as an external observer would. Given the choice of watching a videotape of themselves or one of someone else, they choose to watch themselves (Robins and Oliver, 1997). To them the experience is pure pleasure.

Another thing we can do is control the motives we assign to someone else's behavior. If we continually attribute their behavior to ill will or rejection, we will be in a constant state of negative arousal and the contagion of negative emotion will have begun. If instead we give the person the benefit of the doubt and assume that perhaps he has had a bad day and really means no disrespect, we will have muted the adverse effects of the behavior on ourselves. Of course, this solution is good only up to a point. If the other person continues to engage in annoying behaviors in spite of our best efforts to point out how annoying the behavior is and to control our own reactions, then we must find other solutions.

If you repeatedly do something that others find annoying, you, too, can improve the situation: you can be more discriminating in your choice of someone to interact with. As I mentioned in chapter 2, some people are better than others at listening to complaints. These are the people a chronic complainer should seek out. Similarly, some people are better than others at giving reassurance. Some are less offended than others by breaches of propriety. And we know that two people can respond to the same kind of teasing in very different ways. So if you seem to be unable to stop being annoying, at least be annoying to the right person, the one who will give you the feedback you want.

Every Cloud Has a Silver Lining

Although all annoying behaviors seem to threaten the victim's need to belong, a perpetrator may actually be doing whatever you find annoying with the thought of ultimately improving your relationship. When people nag and complain, they are usually trying to change behaviors that are proving detrimental to their relationship. Although the partner may view the incessant complaining as threatening and annoying, in fact, its purpose is generally to improve the quality of the relationship.

Or take worry. In moderation, worry is a good thing. It alerts us to potential danger and allows us to plan alternative courses of action in the face of danger. "Better to hear bad news from your own people," Hallowell (1997) points out, "than read about it in someone else's victory speech. The work of anticipating bad news—i.e., the work of worry—can be useful" (39). Up to a point, worry can be energizing. Think of a time when you had to give a presentation or take a test. As your worry and anxiety increase, up to a point, so does your performance. It is only when your worry becomes excessive that it interferes with performance. In addition, Hallowell points out, worry can be stimulating and exciting to the worrier. This is not to say that people enjoy worrying, but they may find it distracting.

Coping

The annoying behaviors of other people are among the many stressors we face as we move through life. Like other stressors, they can have both psychological and physical consequences. To reduce the negative impact of stressors, we must find ways to cope. Clearly there are individual differences in the ways people cope with stressors. Whereas some people ride the waves very well, other people are so debilitated by the constant need to cope that their functioning is impaired. There are both positive and negative ways of coping. People who ruminate about others' annoying behaviors, continually get angry about them, or take offense at them will cope ineffectively and surely experience problems in their personal lives and in their relationships. On the other hand, individuals who can find meaning in these annoyances, who can infuse humor into others' annoyingness and learn to forgive them, will find the behaviors less stressful and will experience significantly fewer difficulties (Snyder and Pulvers, 2001).

• • • • • • • • •
References

Abrams, J., and C. Zweig. 1991. *Meeting the Shadow: The Hidden Power of the Dark Side of Human Nature.* Los Angeles: J. P. Tarcher.

American Psychiatric Association. 1994. *Diagnostic and Statistical Manual of Mental Disorders.* 4th ed. (DSM-IV.) Washington, D.C.

Amodeo, J. 1994. *Love and Betrayal.* New York: Ballantine.

Andersson, L. M., and C. M. Pearson. 1999. "Tit for tat? The spiraling effect of incivility in the workplace." *Academy of Management Review* 24:452–72.

Ayduk, O., G. Downey, and M. Kim. 2001. "Rejection sensitivity and depression in women." *Personality and Social Psychology Bulletin* 27:868–77.

"Bad-mannered cell phone users disrupt conferences." 1999, Oct. 22. *Business Courier* (Cincinnati) 16:50–56.

Baron, R. A., and J. H. Neuman. 1996. "Workplace violence and workplace aggression: Evidence on the relative frequency and potential causes." *Aggressive Behavior* 22:161–73.

Barry, D. 1996, Oct. 5. "Pet peeves are ear-splitting Harleys and constant restaurant complaints." *Asheville Citizen Times,* D2.

Bass, C. D. 1999, Nov. 23. "Workplace rudeness on rise, Columbia, S.C.–based research firm finds." *Dallas Morning News.*

Baumeister, R. F. 1991. *Meanings of Life.* New York: Guilford.

———. 1997. *Evil: Inside Human Violence and Cruelty.* New York: W. H. Freeman.

Baumeister, R. F., B. J. Bushman, and W. K. Campbell. 2000. "Self-esteem, narcissism, and aggression: Does violence result from low self-esteem or from threatened egotism?" *Current Directions in Psychological Science* 9: 26–29.

Baumeister, R. F., and W. K. Campbell. 1999. "The intrinsic appeal of evil: Sadism, sensational thrills, and threatened egotism." *Personality and Social Psychology Bulletin* 3:210–21.

Baumeister, R. F., and E. E. Jones. 1978. "When self-presentation is constrained by the target's knowledge: Consistency and compensation." *Journal of Personality and Social Psychology* 36:608–18.

Baumeister, R. F., and M. R. Leary. 1995. "The need to belong: Desire for interpersonal attachments as a fundamental human motivation." *Psychological Bulletin* 117:497–529.

Baxter, L. A., M. Mazanec, J. Nicholson, G. Pittman, K. Smith, and L. West. 1997. "Everyday loyalties and betrayals in personal relationships." *Journal of Social and Personal Relationships* 14:655–78.

Berne, E. 1964. *Games People Play.* New York: Ballantine.

Birney, B. 1992. *Oh, Bother! Somebody's Grumpy!* Disney's Winnie-the-Pooh Helping Hands book. Racine, Wis.: Western Publishing Company.

Borkovec, T. D. 1994. "The nature, functions, and origins of worry." In G. C. L. Davey and F. Tallis, eds., *Worrying: Perspectives on Theory, Assessment, and Treatment,* 5–33. New York: Wiley.

Bornstein, R. F., A. B. Krukonis, K. A. Manning, C. C. Mastrosimone, and S. C. Rossner. 1993. "Interpersonal dependency and health service utilization in a college student sample." *Journal of Social and Clinical Psychology* 12:262–79.

Boyd, L. 1997, Apr. 13. "How parents can say no to whining." *Asheville Citizen Times,* D5.

Brown, J. D. 1991. "Accuracy and bias in self-knowledge." In C. R. Snyder and D. F. Forsyth, eds., *Handbook of Social and Clinical Psychology: The Health Perspective,* 158–78. Elmsford, N.Y.: Pergamon.

Buchinger, E. T. 1999, Sept. 5. "Are you being civil?" *Asheville Citizen Times,* C1.

Cameron, P. 1969. "Frequency and kinds of words in various social settings, or What the hell's going on?" *Pacific Sociological Review* 3:101–04.

Carroll, R. P. 1931. "Snobbishness and egotism." *Journal of Educational Sociology* 5:167–71.

Carter, S. L. 1998. *Civility: Manners, Morals, and the Etiquette of Democracy.* New York: Basic Books.

Cohen-Posey, K. 1995. *How to Handle Bullies, Teasers, and Other Meanies.* Highland City, Fla.: Rainbow Books.

Collins, R. L. 1996. "For better or worse: The impact of upward social comparison on self-evaluations." *Psychological Bulletin* 119:51–69.

Coovert, M. D., and G. D. Reeder. 1990. "Negativity effects in impression formation: The role of unit formation and schematic expectations." *Journal of Personality and Social Psychology* 26:49–62.

Coyne, J. C., R. C. Kessler, M. Tal, J. Turnbull, C. B. Wortman, and J. F. Creden. 1987. "Living with a depressed person." *Journal of Consulting and Clinical Psychology* 55:347–52.

Cunningham, M. R., A. P. Barbee, and P. B. Druen. 1997. "Social allergens and the reactions that they produce: Escalation of annoyance and disgust in love and work." In R. M. Kowalski, ed., *Aversive Interpersonal Behaviors,* 189–214. New York: Plenum.

Cupach, W. R. 1994. "Social predicaments." In W. R. Cupach and B. H. Spitzberg, eds., *The Dark Side of Interpersonal Communications,* 159–80. Hillsdale, N.J.: Lawrence Erlbaum.

Dale, K., and R. F. Baumeister. 1999. "Self-regulation and psychopathology." In R. M. Kowalski and M. R. Leary, eds., *The Social Psychology of Emotional and Behavioral Problems,* 139–66. Washington, D.C.: American Psychological Association.

Deluga, R. J. 1997. "Relationships among American presidential charismatic leadership, narcissism, and rated performance." *Leadership Quarterly* 8:49–65.

Denollet, J. 1991. "Negative affectivity and repressive coping: Pervasive influence on self-reported mood, health, and coronary-prone behavior." *Psychosomatic Medicine* 53:538–56.

Denollet, J., S. U. Sys, N. Stroobant, H. Rombouts, T. C. Gillebert, and D. L. Brutsaert. 1996. "Personality as independent predictor of long-term mortality in patients with cornonary heart disease." *Lancet* 347:417–21.

DePaulo, Bella M., D. A. Kashy, S. E. Kirkendol, M. M. Wyer, and J. A. Epstein. 1996. "Lying in everyday life." *Journal of Personality and Social Psychology* 70:979–95.

Downey, G., and S. I. Feldman. 1996. "Implications of rejection sensitivity for intimate relationships." *Journal of Personality and Social Psychology* 70: 1327–43.

Downey, G., A. L. Freitas, B. Michaelis, and H. Khouri. 1998. "The self-fulfilling prophecy in close relationships: Rejection sensitivity and rejection by romantic partners." *Journal of Personality and Social Psychology* 75: 545–60.

Elangovan, A. R., and D. C. Shapiro. 1998. "Betrayal of trust in organizations." *Academy of Management Review* 23:547–66.

Elkind, D. 1991. "Instrumental narcissism in parents." *Bulletin of the Menninger Clinic* 55:299–307.

Emmons, R. A. 1987. "Narcissism: Theory and measurement." *Journal of Personality and Social Psychology* 52:11–17.

———. 2000. "Personality and forgiveness." In M. E. McCullough, K. I. Pargament, and C. E. Thoresen, eds., *Forgiveness: Theory, Research, and Practice,* 156–75. New York: Guilford.

Exline, J. J., and R. F. Baumeister. 2000. "Expressing forgiveness and repentance: Benefits and barriers." In M. E. McCullough, K. I. Pargament, and C. E. Thoresen, eds., *Forgiveness: Theory, Research, and Practice,* 133–55. New York: Guilford.

Farina, A., D. S. Wheeler, and S. Mehta. 1991. "The impact of an unpleasant and demeaning social interaction." *Journal of Social and Clinical Psychology* 10:351–71.

Folkman, S., and R. S. Lazarus. 1986. "Stress process and depressive symptomology." *Journal of Abnormal Psychology* 95:107–13.

Ford, C. V. 1996. *Lies! Lies! Lies!: The Psychology of Deceit.* Washington, D.C.: American Psychiatric Press.

Frank, J. D., E. Ascher, J. B. Margolin, H. Nash, A. R. Stone, and E. J. Varon. 1952. "Behavioral patterns in early meetings of therapeutic groups." *American Journal of Psychiatry* 108:771–78.

Freud, S. 1914/1957. "On narcissism: An introduction." In S. Freud, *The Standard Edition of the Complete Works of Sigmund Freud,* ed. and trans. J. Strachey et al., 19:12–66. London: Hogarth.

Georgesen, J. C., M. J. Harris, R. Milich, and J. Bosko-Young. 1999. "'Just teasing.': Personality effects on perceptions and life narratives of childhood teasing." *Personality and Social Psychology Bulletin* 25:1254–67.

Gilovich, T., J. Kruger, and K. Savitsky. 1999. "Everyday egocentrism and everyday interpersonal problems." In R. M. Kowalski and M. R. Leary, eds., *The Social Psychology of Emotional and Behavioral Problems: Interfaces of Social and Clinical Psychology,* 69–95. Washington, D.C.: American Psychological Association.

Gilovich, T., V. H. Medvec, and K. Savitsky. 1998. "The spotlight effect in social judgment: An egocentric bias in estimates of the salience of one's actions and appearance." Unpublished manuscript, Cornell University.

Gilovich, T. , K. Savitsky, and V. H. Medvec. 1998. "The illusion of transparency: Biased estimates of others' ability to read our emotional states." *Journal of Personality and Social Psychology* 75:332–46.

Gladwell, M. 2000. *The Tipping Point: How Little Things Can Make a Big Difference*. Boston: Little, Brown.

Goetz, A. 1999, Nov. 26. "Etiquette classes add dose of civility to the workplace." *Business First—Columbus*, 27.

Goffman, E. 1967. *Interaction Ritual: Essays on Face-to-Face Behavior*. New York: Pantheon.

Goldstein, A. P. 1994. *The Ecology of Aggression*. New York: Plenum.

Gottman, J. M. 1994. *Why Marriages Succeed or Fail*. New York: Simon and Schuster.

Griegson, J. 1998. *The Joys of Complaining*. London: Robson.

Grossman, K. N. 1999, Aug. 29. "Who's rude at work? Study shows it's mostly men behaving badly." *Asheville Citizen Times*, A1.

Hallmark, S. W., and R. L. Curtis. 1994. "Arrogance: The public interaction of role claims and role performance." Paper presented at the annual meeting of the Society for the Study of Social Problems.

Hallowell, E. M. 1997. *Worry*. New York: Ballantine.

Held, B. 1999. *Stop Smiling, Start Kvetching*. New York: Audenreed.

Hill, R. W., and G. P. Yousey. 1998. "Adaptive and maladaptive narcissism among university faculty, clergy, politicians, and librarians." *Current Psychology* 17:163–88.

Holland, J. C., and S. Lewis. 1996. "Emotions and cancer: What do we really know?" In D. Goleman and J. Gurin, eds., *Mind/Body Medicine: How to Use Your Mind for Better Health*, 85–109. Yonkers, N.Y.: Consumer Reports Books.

Holmes, J. 1993. *Women, Men, and Politeness*. New York: Longmans.

"Honesty." 1999, January. *Current Health* 22:29–31.

Hoover, J. H., and R. Oliver. 1996. *The Bullying Prevention Handbook*. Bloomington, Ind.: National Educational Service.

Hulme, L. 1994. *Pet Peeves: More than 200 Irritations from Everyday Life*. Fort Worth: Summit Group.

Hwang, Y. G. 1995. "Student apathy, lack of self-responsibility, and false self-esteem are failing American schools." *Education* 115:484–91.

Infante, D. A., R. L. Riddle, C. L. Horvath, and S. A. Tumlin. 1992. "Verbal aggressiveness: Messages and reasons." *Communication Quarterly* 40: 116–26.

Jack, D. 1991. *Silencing the Self.* New York: HarperCollins.

Jay, T. B. 1992. *Cursing in America.* Philadelphia: John Benjamins.

Joiner, T. E., Jr., and G. I. Metalsky. 1995. "A prospective test of an integrative interpersonal theory of depression: A naturalistic study of college roommates." *Journal of Personality and Social Psychology* 69:778–88.

Jones, W. H., and M. P. Burdette. 1994. "Betrayal in relationships." In A. L. Weber and J. H. Harvey, eds., *Perspectives on Close Relationships,* 243–62. Boston: Allyn and Bacon.

Jones, W. H., D. S. Moore, A. Schratter, and L. A. Negel. 2001. "Interpersonal transgressions and betrayals." In R. M. Kowalski, ed., *Behaving Badly: Aversive Behaviors in Interpersonal Relationships,* 233–56. Washington, D.C., American Psychological Association.

Katz, J., and S. R. H. Beach. 1997. "Romance in the crossfire: When do women's depressive symptoms predict partner relationship dissatisfaction?" *Journal of Social and Clinical Psychology* 16:243–58.

Katz, J., S. R. H. Beach, and T. E. Joiner, Jr. 1999. "Contagious depression in dating couples." *Journal of Social and Clinical Psychology* 18:1–13.

Katz, J., and T. E. Joiner, Jr. 2001. "The aversive interpersonal context of depression: Emerging perspectives on depressotypic behavior." In R. M. Kowalski, ed., *Behaving Badly: Aversive Behaviors in Interpersonal Relationships,* 117–47. Washington, D.C.: American Psychological Association.

Kauffman, J. M., and H. J. Burbach. 1998, February. "Creating classroom civility." *Education Digest* 63:12–19.

Kernberg, O. 1975/1985. *Borderline Conditions and Pathological Narcissism.* New York: Jason Aronson.

Kernis, M. H., B. D. Grannemann, and L. C. Barclay. 1989. "Stability and self-esteem as predictors of anger, arousal, and hostility." *Journal of Personality and Social Psychology* 56:1013–1.22.

Kindlon, D., and M. Thompson. 1999. *Raising Cain: Protecting the Emotional Lives of Boys.* New York: Ballantine.

Knapp, M. L., L. Stafford, and J. A. Daly. 1986. "Regrettable messages: Things people wish they hadn't said." *Journal of Communication* 36:40–58.

Kornet, A. 1997. "The truth about lying." *Psychology Today* 30:53–59.

Kowalski, R. M. 1996. "Complaints and complaining: Functions, antecedents, and consequences." *Psychological Bulletin* 119:179–96.

————, ed. 1997. *Aversive Interpersonal Behaviors*. New York: Plenum.

————. 2000. "I was only kidding!': Victims' and perpetrators' perceptions of teasing." *Personality and Social Psychology Bulletin* 26:234–41.

Kowalski, R. M., and C. Cantrell. 2002. "Interpersonal and intrapersonal consequences of complaints." *Representative Research in Social Psychology*, 26:26–33.

Kowalski, R. M., and J. R. Erickson. 1997. "Complaining: What's all the fuss about?" In R. M. Kowalski, ed., *Aversive Interpersonal Behavior*, 91–110. New York: Plenum.

Kowalski, R. M., E. Howerton, and M. McKenzie. 2001. "Permitted disrespect: Teasing in interpersonal interactions." In R. M. Kowalski, ed., *Behaving Badly: Aversive Behaviors in Interpersonal Interactions*, 177–202. Washington, D.C.: American Psychological Association.

Kowalski, R. M., S. Valentine, R. Wilkinson, A. Queen, and B. Sharpe. In press. "Lying, cheating, complaining, and other aversive interpersonal behaviors: A narrative examination of the darker side of relationships." *Journal of Social and Personal Relationships*.

Krantz, M. 1994. *Child Development: Risk and Opportunity*. Belmont, Calif.: Wadsworth.

Leary, M. R. 1995. *Self-Presentation: Impression Management and Interpersonal Behavior*. Dubuque: Brown and Benchmark.

Leary, M. R., R. Bednarski, D. Hammon, and T. Duncan. 1997. "Blowhards, snobs, and narcissists: Interpersonal reactions to excessive egotism." In R. M. Kowalski, ed., *Aversive Interpersonal Behaviors*, 111–31. New York: Plenum.

Leary, M. R., and D. L. Downs. 1995. "Interpersonal functions of the self-esteem motive: The self-esteem system as a sociometer." In M. Kernis, ed., *Efficiency, Agency, and Self-Esteem*, 123–44. New York: Plenum.

Leary, M. R., and R. M. Kowalski. 1990. "Impression management: A literature review and two-factor model." *Psychological Bulletin* 107:34–47.

Leary, M. R., and C. A. Springer. 2001. "Hurt feelings: The neglected emotion." In R. M. Kowalski, ed., *Behaving Badly: Aversive Behaviors in Interpersonal Relationships*, 151–75. Washington, D.C.: American Psychological Association.

Lee, K., and H. J. Ross. 1997. "The concept of lying in adolescents and young adults: Testing Sweetser's folkloristic model." *Merrill-Palmer Quarterly* 43:255–70.

Leo, J. 1996, Apr. 22. "Foul words, foul culture." *U.S. News & World Report.*

Malmquist, C. P. 1996. *Homicide: A Psychiatric Perspective.* Washington, D.C.: American Psychiatric Press.

"Many drivers confess their faults in poll." 1999, Dec. 20. *Auto Week,* 8–11.

Marano, H. E. 1998. *Why Doesn't Anybody Like Me?* New York: Morrow.

Marks, J. 1996, Apr. 22. "The American uncivil wars: How crude, rude, and obnoxious behavior has replaced good manners and why that hurts our politics and culture." *U.S. News & World Report,* 66–72.

Mathews-Coleman, D., K. Kelley, K. Mooney, and R. Kowalski. 1997. "Complaining in the media: An examination of letters to the editor." Paper presented at the meeting of the Southeastern Psychological Association, Atlanta.

McCafferty, D. 1999, Dec. 10–12. "Got a complaint? 5 ways to get results online." *USA Weekend,* 12–13.

McKenzie, E. C. 1980. *14,000 Quips and Quotes for Writers and Speakers.* New York: Wings Books.

Metts, S. 1998. "Relational transgressions." In W. R. Cupach and B. H. Spitzberg, eds., *The Dark Side of Interpersonal Communication,* 217–39. Hillsdale, N.J.: Lawrence Erlbaum.

———. 1999. "An exploratory investigation of deception in close relationships." *Journal of Social and Personal Relationships* 6:495–512.

Metts, S., and W. R. Cupach. 1989. "Situational influences on the use of remedial strategies in embarrassing predicaments." *Communication Monographs* 56:151–62.

Meyer, T. J., M. L. Miller, R. L. Metzger, and T. D. Borkovec. 1990. "Development and validation of the Penn State Worry Questionnaire." *Behaviour Research and Therapy* 28:487–95.

Miller, R. S. 1997. "We always hurt the ones we love: Aversive interactions in close relationships." In R. M. Kowalski, ed., *Aversive Interpersonal Behaviors,* 11–29. New York: Plenum.

———. 2001. "Breaches of propriety." In R. M. Kowalski, ed., *Behaving Badly: Aversive Behaviors in Interpersonal Relationships,* 29–58. Washington, D.C.: American Psychological Association.

Millon, T. 1981. *Disorders of Personality: DSM III, Axis II.* New York: Wiley.

Mooney, A., R. Cresser, and P. Blatchford. 1991. "Children's views on teasing and fighting in junior schools." *Educational Research* 33:103–12.

Muraven, M., and R. F. Baumeister. 2000. "Self-regulation and depletion of limited resources: Does self-control resemble a muscle?" *Psychological Bulletin* 126:247–59.

Naughton, K. 2000, Mar. 6. "Tired of smile-free service?" *Newsweek*, 44.

Neuman, J. H., and R. A. Baron. 1997. "Aggression in the workplace." In R. A. Giacalone and J. Greenberg, eds., *Antisocial Behavior in Organizations*, 37–67. Thousand Oaks, Calif.: Sage.

Olweus, D. 1993. *Bullying at School: What We Know and What We Can Do.* Oxford: Blackwell.

Oswald, H., L. Krappman., I. Chowdhuri, and M. von Salisch. 1987. "Gaps and bridges: Interactions between girls and boys in elementary school." *Sociological Studies of Child Development* 2:205–23.

Papps, B. P., and R. E. O'Carroll. 1998. "Extremes of self-esteem and narcissism and the experience and expression of anger and aggression." *Aggressive Behavior* 24:421–38.

Pearce, J. 1989. *Fighting, Teasing, and Bullying: Simple and Effective Ways to Help Your Child.* Wellingborough: Thorsons.

Pearson, C. M., L. M. Andersson, and C. L. Porath. 2000. "Assessing and attacking workplace incivility." *Organizational Dynamics* 29:123–38.

Peterson, C. 1996. "Deception in intimate relationships." *International Journal of Psychology* 31:179–88.

Powers, J. 1996. *Eeyore's Gloomy Little Instruction Book.* New York: Dutton.

Raskin, R. N., and C. S. Hall. 1979. "A narcissistic personality inventory." *Psychological Reports* 45:590.

Reddy, V. 1991. "Playing with others' expectations: Teasing and mucking about in the first year." In A. Whiten, ed., *Natural Theories of Mind,* 143–58. Cambridge, Mass.: Basil Blackwell.

Rigby, K. 1997. "What children tell us about bullying in schools." *Children Australia* 22:28–34.

Robins, R. W., and J. P. Oliver. 1997. "Effects of visual perspective and narcissism on self-perception: Is seeing believing?" *Psychological Science* 8:37–42.

Robinson, K. 1997, Apr. 13. "Don't get mad if you're mistreated—complain!" *Asheville Citizen Times,* C1.

Rook, K. S. 1998. "Investigating the positive and negative sides of personal relationships: Through a lens darkly?" In B. H. Spitzberg and W. R.

Cupach, eds., *The Dark Side of Close Relationships*, 369–93. Mahwah, N.J.: Erlbaum.

Ross, D. M. 1996. *Childhood Bullying and Teasing*. Alexandria, Va.: American Counseling Association.

Ross, M., and F. Sicoly. 1979. Egocentric biases in availability and attribution." *Journal of Personality and Social Psychology* 37:322–36.

"The rule of honesty for a successful marriage." 1999, Sept. 8. <http://www.marriagebuilders.com/graphic/mbi3800_honesty.html>

Rustigen, M. 1996, Aug. 1. "Anger, egotism drive 'heroes' to crime." *Winston-Salem Journal*, A10.

Sampson, O. 1999, Nov. 15. "A darned short history of swearing." *Gazette* (Colorado Springs).

Schlesinger, L. B. 1998. "Pathological narcissism and serial homicide: Review and case study." *Current Psychology* 17:212–21.

Schutz, A. 1998. "Audience perceptions of politicians' self-presentational behaviors concerning their own abilities." *Journal of Social Psychology* 138: 173–88.

Shapiro, J. P., R. F. Baumeister, and J. W. Kessler. 1991. "A three-component model of children's teasing: Aggression, humor, and ambiguity." *Journal of Social and Clinical Psychology* 10:459–72.

Simmons, R. 2002. *Odd Girl Out*. New York: Harcourt.

"Skies can be treacherous for airline crews and passengers amid incidents of air rage." 2000, Jan. 16. *Canadian Press.*

"Slay suspect reportedly took out policy on infant." 1999, July 4. *Boston Globe*, A15.

Snyder, C. R., and K. M. Pulvers. 2001. "Copers coping with stress: Two against one." In C. R. Snyder, ed., *Coping with Stress: Effective People and Processes*, 285–301. New York: Oxford University Press.

Soyer, R. B., J. L. Rovenpor, and R. E. Kopelman. 1999. "Narcissism and achievement motivation as related to three facets of the sales role: Attraction, satisfaction, and performance." *Journal of Business and Psychology* 14:285–304.

Stone, M. H. 1998. "Normal narcissism: An etiological and ethological perspective." In E. F. Ronningstam et al., eds., *Disorders of Narcissism: Diagnostic, Clinical, and Empirical Implications*, 7–28. Washington, D.C.: American Psychiatric Press.

Storms, M. D., and K. D. McCaul. 1976. "Attribution processes and emotional exacerbation of dysfunctional behavior." In J. H. Harvey, W. J.

Ickes, and R. F. Kidd, eds., *New Directions in Attribution Research*, 1:143–64. Hillsdale, N.J.: Lawrence Erlbaum.

Stover, D. 1999, January. "Raising students' civil behavior." *Education Digest* 64:11–14.

Swann, W. B., Jr., and J. K. Bosson. 1999. "The flip side of the reassurance-seeking coin: The partner's perspective." *Psychological Inquiry* 10:302–04.

"Taxi driver's swearing 'not uncivil.' " 1999, July 14. *Hong Kong Standard*.

Taylor, S. E., and J. D. Brown. 1988. "Illusion and well-being: A social psychological perspective on mental health." *Psychological Bulletin* 103:193–210.

Taylor, S. E., L. A. Peplau, and D. O. Sears. 2000. *Social Psychology*, 10th ed. Upper Saddle River, N.J.: Prentice-Hall.

Thernstrom, A. 1999, Summer. "Courting disorder in the schools." *Public Interest* 136:18–35.

Thompson, J. K., J. Cattarin, B. Fowler, and E. Fisher. 1995. "The Perception of Teasing Scale (POTS): A revision and extension of the Physical Appearance Related Teasing Scale (PARTS)." *Journal of Personality Assessment* 65:146–57.

"Three boys assaulted while playing in sand pit." 1998, Dec. 24. Associated Press State and Local Wire.

Twenge, J. M. 2000. "The age of anxiety: The birth cohort change in anxiety and neuroticism." *Journal of Personality and Social Psychology* 79:1007–21.

"Unruly passenger forced plane to land in Winnipeg." 2000, Jan. 12. *Canadian Press*.

Watts, A. 1998. "'You are such a tease!': Identifying and describing the chronic teaser." Master's thesis, Western Carolina University.

Windsor, P. 1999, Apr. 23. "What do companies pay for workplace rudeness?" *Washington Business Journal*, 52–55.

Winters, A. M., and S. Duck. 2001. "You ****!: Swearing as an aversive and a relational activity." In R. M. Kowalski, ed., *Behaving Badly: Aversive Behaviors in Interpersonal Relationships*, 59–77. Washington, D.C.: American Psychological Association.

Yalom, I. D. 1985. *The Theory and Practice of Group Psychotherapy*. New York: Basic Books.

Zoroya, G. 1999, Aug. 3. "Techno annoyed." *Asheville Citizen Times*, C1.

• • • • • • • • •

Index